LATINX SUPERHEROES IN MAINSTREAM COMICS

Latinx Pop Culture

SERIES EDITORS

Frederick Luis Aldama and Arturo J. Aldama

LATINX SUPERHEROES IN MAINSTREAM COMICS

Frederick Luis Aldama

Foreword by John Jennings

Afterword by Javier Hernandez

THE UNIVERSITY OF
ARIZONA PRESS

TUCSON

The University of Arizona Press
www.uapress.arizona.edu

Printed in the United States of America

ISBN-13: 978-0-8165-3708-2 (paper)

Cover design by Leigh McDonald
Cover art: *America Chavez* by John Jennings

Publication of this book is made possible in part by the proceeds of a permanent
endowment created with the assistance of a Challenge Grant from the National
Endowment for the Humanities, a federal agency.

Library of Congress Cataloging-in-Publication Data
Names: Aldama, Frederick Luis, 1969– author. | Jennings, John, 1970– writer of fore-
    word. | Hernandez, Javier, 1966– writer of afterword.
Title: Latinx superheroes in mainstream comics / Frederick Luis Aldama ; foreword
    by John Jennings ; afterword by Javier Hernandez.
Description: Tucson : The University of Arizona Press, 2017. | Series: Latinx pop cul-
    ture | Includes bibliographical references and index.
Identifiers: LCCN 2017010449 | ISBN 9780816537082 (pbk. : alk. paper)
Subjects: LCSH: Comic books, strips, etc.—United States—History and criticism.
    | Hispanic Americans in literature. | Hispanic Americans in popular culture. |
    Superheroes. | Comic books, strips, etc.—Social aspects—United States. | Popular
    culture—United States.
Classification: LCC PN6725 .A37 2017 | DDC 741.5/352968073—dc23 LC record
    available at https://lccn.loc.gov/2017010449

♾ This paper meets the requirements of ANSI/NISO Z39.48-1992 (Permanence of
Paper).

For Corina Isabel,

my very own Latinx comic book aficionado in the making

"You have the right not to utter racial, ethnic or genetic slurs."
—ANGELA DEL TORO, *WHITE TIGER*

*"Samuel Alejandro!... ¿Donde te habias metido?... Acabas de salir del hospital...
Mom, English por favor."*
—SAM ALEJANDRO AS THE NEW NOVA, *MARVEL NOW! NOVA*

*"¡Ay dios! America Chavez! Stop this running around at once. You must come home...
We saved the world and left you a utopia... And you run away from it!"*
—THE TWO MAMAS OF LGBT TEEN AMERICA CHAVEZ, *YOUNG AVENGERS*

CONTENTS

IT'S HARD BEING INVISIBLE

A Foreword

Growing up black, poor, and Southern made sure of my imperceptibility to the mainstream. So, like most invisible people, I turned to stories in popular media to start to build some sense of self to reflect back to my burgeoning psyche. Despite integration, the school I attended was pretty much 100 percent African American. However, I didn't really think about race in the media I consumed. My favorite comic book superheroes were all white, cisgender, straight men from large cities. They were basically the opposite of me. I didn't realize this at the time, but that's the truth of being born into the United States' socially constructed identity matrices we are presented with even before we are born in the USA.

My mother introduced me to reading at an early age. She was an English literature major, and she had plenty of her college books around. She invested heavily, as much as she could, in my learning habits, and I fell in love with knowledge. However, when she bought me my first comics, *The Mighty Thor* and *Spider-Man*, little did she know that she was starting an obsession that would fuel my artwork, my career, and my life.

My favorite superhero is Daredevil. A tough Irish bookworm from Hell's Kitchen, New York City; a place I had never been to and had no real conception of was my index for identity. I related to his poverty. I related to him being taunted by bullies. I related to him feeling isolated and odd. The thing I loved most about the character wasn't the superpowers that he gained later. I loved his grit—his tenacity to keep going. I learned about how to struggle through that character, and not through a black character. Luke Cage, The Falcon, and Black Panther were cool enough, but they were never written in a manner with which I could connect. I could understand what it meant to go hungry, to feel small, and to want to succeed. I *was* Matt Murdock. I honestly didn't understand the weight of what it meant to be codified as "black" until January 23, 1977. That was the first airing of the original ABC miniseries *Roots*, based on the Alex Haley novel. My complexion is much lighter than that of my grandfather's, but his skin looked like the skin of these people who were being hurt, shamed, enslaved, and controlled. I then realized through subsequent viewings that my lighter skin was due to two or more races "mixing." The notion that a country that I pledged allegiance to every day in school would be based on something as horrible as chattel slavery broke my seven-year-old mind. That realization hurt me deeply. Those representations changed my life. My eyes saw my school, my teachers, and the absence of white students in our classes very differently after that miniseries ended. Comics became even more of an escape after I realized not only my social status, but also my "inferior" status as a black person in the South.

During graduate school at the University of Illinois at Urbana-Champaign, I began to realize my political attitudes toward representation, comics, and identity. I was coming closer to the perspectives that I now hold dear. It wasn't until my time teaching at that same institution a few years later that I recognized my calling. I began collaborating on independent comics and creating comic book communities inclusive of intersectional identities: race, ethnicity, sexuality, gender, and class. It was also the first time that I met Frederick Aldama. Little did I know that I was meeting not just a kindred spirit but also an inspirational figure, in my own pursuit of equity.

My favorite character, Daredevil, had augmented senses that gave his perceptions no "blind spots." All of his senses were heightened to superhuman levels, and he possessed a kind of "radar" that enabled him to do things that "normal" humans couldn't. His "handicap" was his own character and even his Catholic faith. He is a very complex and compelling protagonist in that regard. You see, we all have blind spots. There are always spaces that are basically the shape of an absence in our worldviews. They behave like that space that Stephen King described in his novel, *The Dead Zone*. It's a space that is incomplete. It is also a space for potential change.

As a black scholar, it almost seems cliché for me to study black identity, black history, and black cultural production. My own "me-search" has taken me far and wide talking about comics, stereotypes, social justice, and the power of symbolic annihilation. That focus can also become a blindness. You can become so intensely knowledgeable about the depth, width, and shape of your own navel that you can't see anything else. You can see this happening with a patriarchal lens, a lens based in class, or even one that comes from a particular area of study or faith. That expertise can be a weakness. That notion is one of the reasons why I love interdisciplinary research and critically creative exercises. It's one of the reasons why I love what Frederick does with his passion. He strives to bring everyone together through his fiction, his social justice work, and his scholarship. I learn something every time I hear him speak. My blind spots get smaller after every conversation.

This book goes in depth regarding part of a tradition of storytelling that has excluded just as much as it has empowered. It shines a light on creators and characters that were just in the peripheral vision of popular culture. You have to understand that to not show something is just as powerful as showing something.

Our country is very good at erasing its own history and its own citizens. It's part of the American Way. There's an idealized notion around what an American looks like and, therefore, what the American superhero looks like. On the other hand, the nation touts its independence, acceptance, and multiculturalism as an example to the world. The oppressed know the score. We understand that it's not one or the other. It's both. We also understand that media controls the mind's eye of the population. It's vital to see oneself as a hero, a villain, a savior, and a sidekick. We all have a spectrum of experiences locked within us. Comics and other popular media, when done well, can help unlock a plethora of experiences. It's one of the reasons why I love making comic books and helping others do the same.

Yes, it's hard being invisible, but sometimes it's even harder to see. Ironically, the truth is usually always right next to us comfortably nestled in our blind spots. We don't have a radar-sense like Matt Murdock, but we can have the foresight to listen to each other, to allow for people to be human, and to step outside of our comfort zones. Did I mention that Daredevil's nickname is "The Man Without Fear"? He's so lucky. In the real world we have to contend with our fears and best them if possible. That means putting out our stories and supporting each other's narratives. That's one of the reasons why Frederick, Ricardo Padilla (creator and cofounder of the Latino Comix Expo), and I co-founded Sol-Con: The Brown and Black Comix Expo—to retool perceptions of black and brown creators and characters in our society. The energy that pulses through Aldama's *Latinx Superheroes in Mainstream Comics* is one big step in this direction. It's one big step for black and brown kind.

John Jennings, Professor
of Media and Cultural
Studies, University of
California, Riverside

PREFACE AND ACKNOWLEDGMENTS

This is a book about Latinx superheroes in mainstream comic book storyworlds. While printed comic books (DC and Marvel mostly) take up the lion's share of space in the book, I do clear space to discuss Latinx comic book superheroes in animation, TV, and film. Hence, the use of the expansive concept of comic book *storyworlds*. I also see this book as an initial step in giving some definition to further work in this area. This book is a scaffolding of sorts that I hope will signal to others the need for scholarly work in this area as we continue to co-create the ever-evolving, tessellating edifice that is Latinx comics.

This is not my first flight into this arena. I knew when I published *Your Brain on Latino Comics* (2009) that there was more recovery and interpretive work to be done—in the independent *and* the mainstream scenes. With *Your Brain on Latino Comics* I wanted to throw wide the doors and windows to the significant presence of comics by and about Latinos in all genres. Representations of U.S. Latinos in comic books and U.S. Latino creators of comics had yet to be systematically identified and interpreted, so writing this first book seemed a tall order, to say the least. And I was in desperate need of fresh air. There were all these interpretive studies on comic books, but none focused on Latinos. In that book, then, I felt like a bit of a homegrown superhero, having built up some visual-verbal interpretive muscle and know-how. As a teacher and scholar I could kick some villainous cultural gatekeeper butt *and* throw open doors to free all variety of Latinos kept under lock and key in the prison house of a white-dominant culture.

Latinx Superheroes in Mainstream Comics aims to blast wider other doors. It aims to explore more deeply and systematically the storyworld spaces inhabited by brown superheroes in mainstream comic book storyworlds: print comic books, animation, TV, and film. As with all of my interpretive cultural work, I seek to make visible (and let loose) the otherwise occluded and shackled. I aim to shed some light on how creators (authors, artists, animators, and directors) *make* storyworlds that feature Latinos. I aim to distinguish between those that we can and should evaluate as well-done and those we can and should evaluate as not well-done. We can understand better how some superhero comic book storyworlds are willfully created in ways that *make* new our perception, thought, and feeling about Latinos and how others fail to do so.

I focus on print comic books, animation, TV, and film because, well, this is where the superhero lives. These are the media where we consume superhero stories—and in film, more than ever. Indeed, it is not only a view to the Latino content and comic book form that links these different storytelling formats. It's a response to the way these storytelling formats have grown up *together*, sharing and borrowing shaping devices from one another. That is, we can learn much about the different shaping devices (techniques) used in printed comics, animation, TV, and film to distill and reconstruct *real* Latinos.

○○○

Latinos in superhero comic books storyworlds spring from the foundational drive to create on the part of authors, artists, animators, and directors—and to *co-create* in our imaginations as readers and viewers. In this spirit, in writing this book I keep centrally in mind that within human behavior we have four kinds of relationships: (1) between humans and nature; (2) between humans and the tools or instruments that we create to modify nature; (3) between one human and other humans that make up society; (4) between humans and our tools *and* other humans from an aesthetic point of view. When Rhode Montijo uses the shaping tools of drawing to create his superhero child protagonist, Pablo, he distills, then reconstructs, the aesthetically attractive features of infants—the geometric shape of the circle (head and eyes) along with triangles (the diagonal and straight lines used to foreshorten the small body frame)—to trigger a reflex response in us of tenderness and empathy.

Of course, there's nothing in the DNA, say, of the geometric shapes used. It's that these shapes that we see every day with real infants and their big heads and small bodies have, by convention, grown reflex responses of tenderness and empathy. Rhode's creation of a child superhero (one who dies on earth, then makes

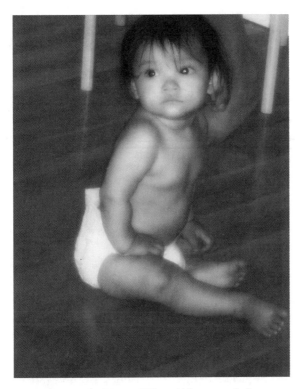

Figure 1. Photograph of Corina Villena-Aldama as an infant.

his way through the underworld of Mictlán, encountering characters like Quetzal and the *luchador* ghost El Calambre) allows him to quickly establish a specific emotive and cognitive relationship between the character and the viewer. Rhode uses geometric shapes to efficiently communicate a sense of the character. Rhode creates a character with an aesthetic intention and contemplation.

Put otherwise, Rhode distills, then reconstructs, from the building blocks of reality (infants and pre-Columbian history and myth) to make an object (comic book and character) that establishes an aesthetic relationality with us. He doesn't provide a research document about infant size and growth scale. He doesn't provide an archive of Mesoamerican history. What Rhode does is create a superhero storyworld that makes new our perception, thought, and feeling.

Of course, not all authors, artists, and directors choose to give shape to Latinos and their respective storyworlds in ways that

Figure 2. Rhode Montijo's Pablo's Inferno.

seek to modify our understanding *and* relationship to the world. As I will explore herein, there are many mainstream creators of Latinx superheroes who slip into the laziness of shallow, denigrating stereotypes.

○○○

Just as we have seen a steady advance in the technologies of making comics from coloring to drawing and the like, there have also been moments when sociohistorical circumstances have been such that comics have been nearly stopped in their tracks; we see the same with animation, when Saturday morning cartoons, too, were considered an eroding force in the strong moral fortitude of the United States. That is, making Latinx superheroes in mainstream comic book storyworlds exists in time and place. Just as the creators are shaped by political, social, and historical circumstances, so, too, are their creations. We know well from the history of the censorship that hit comics and cartoons, with the most draconian measures brought on as a result of Frederic Wertham and a series of congressional hearings in the 1950s that led to the enacting of censorship policies such as the Comic's Code and much later the Children's Television Act. Betwixt and between the passing of these big historical censorship measures there existed and continues to exist a pervasive, pernicious, subterranean eliding and erasing of Latinos, superhero or otherwise. A relative handful of Latinos makes up the superhero comic print world, with even fewer appearing in animation, TV, and film.

The aim of this book is twofold: First, to archive the representation of Latinos in mainstream comic book *storyworlds*. Given that Latinos have appeared most in print comics, this first part of the book takes up the most room out of the four storytelling formats discussed: comic books, animation, TV, and film. Excavating the representational archive bookends *Latinx Superheroes in Mainstream Comics*.

Second, I consider that reading comics or viewing comic book films involves our active *co-creation* (albeit guided) of the storyworld. Each of the respective comic book media explored (in-print, film, animation, and TV) uses different shaping devices to guide how we gap-fill a character, event, or plot—the storyworld globally. Creative teams realize their storyworlds with their own respective narrative shaping devices (panels with in-print comics, lighting and lensing with film, for instance) in ways that invite readers and audiences to imagine with *and* beyond what's in front of them. The careful use of geometric shaping devices in the making of two dimensional, static in-print comics can and do lead readers to experience a kinetic movement between panels and within panels. The careful use of auditory shaping devices in film, animation, and TV shows can infuse a sense of the superheroic (and supervillainy) even before a character *acts* omnipotently. The shaping devices of any given medium invite this plugging-in and interfacing with any given Latinx superhero storyworld. They invite us to co-create in ways that can and do move audiences beyond the limitations of the page, silver screen, animation, or prime-time TV show. Keep in mind, and this will become clear especially in chapter 3 of this book, that there are many such superhero storyworlds that fall short, especially when it comes to the reconstruction of Latinos as superheroes.

○○○

I take a brief pause to offer shout-outs to my fellow interpretive crusaders of all Latino *cultura* that *pops*: José Alaniz, Arturo Aldama, Stacey Alex, Paul Allatson, Cecilia Aragon, Mary Beltrán, Charles Ramírez Berg, Monica Brown, William A. Calvo-Quiros, Melissa Castillo-Garsow, Norma Cantú, Nicholas Centino, Ben Chappell, Osvaldo Cleger, David Colón, Ben Chappell, Fabio Chee, Marivel T. Danielson, Mauricio Espinoza, Laura Fernández, Camilla Fojas, Kathryn M. Frank, Enrique García, Jorge J. González, Rachel V Gonzalez-Martin, Matthew Goodwin, Isabel Molina-Guzmán,

Charles Hatfield, Ellie D. Hernandez, Héctor Fernández l'Hoeste, Jorge Iber, Zachary Ingle, Guisela Latorre, John Leaños, Stephanie Lewthwaite, Francisco Lomelí, Richard Alexander Lou, Stacy I. Macías, Desirée Martin, Pancho McFarland, Cruz Medina, Isabel Millán, Amelia María de la Luz Montes, Paula Moya, William Nericcio, William Orchard, Sue J. Kim, Paloma Martínez-Cruz, Bonnie Opliger, Danielle Orozco, Ricardo Padilla, Juan Poblete, Rocio Prado, Ryan Rashotte, Cristina Rivera, Ricky T. Rodriguez, Theresa Rojas, Gabriela Sanchez, Ilan Stavans, Samuel Saldívar, the Bros Saldívar, Jorge Santos, Lourdes Torres, and Silvio Torres-Sailant.

I pause, too, for some shout-outs to my fellow Latinx comic book creators and animators: Lalo Alcaraz, Jorge Aguirre, Victor Avilla, Candy Briones, Natacha Bustos, José Cabrera, Hector Cantu, Mark Campos, Jaime Crespo, Richard Dominguez, Ulises Fernandez, Frank Espinosa, Jandro Gamboa, Eric Garcia, Jason González, Crystal Gonzalez, John González, Raúl Gonzalez III, Leigh Anna Grace, Raquel Grisales, Israel Francisco Haros Lopez, Adam Hernandez, Javier Hernandez, Los Bros Hernandez, David Herrera, Andrew Huerta, Myra Lara, Alberto Ledesma, Leigh Luna, Carlos Benjamin Madrigal, Liz Mayorga, Laura Molina, Randy Montanez, Rhode Montijo, Alex Olivas, Dave Ortega, Axel Ortiz, Amber Padilla, Daniel Parada, Ricardo Padilla, Breena Nuñez Peralta, Carlos Perez, Jimmy Portillo, Jules Rivera, Cristy C. Road, Fernando Rodriguez, Grasiela Rodriguez, Hector Rodriguez, Jason Rodriguez, Octavio Rodriguez, Theresa Rojas, Naomi Romero, Rafael Rosado, Carlos Saldaña, Julio Salgado, Tony Sandoval, Wilfred Santiago, Serenity Serseción, Christopher Sotomayer, Sam Teer, Viko, Lila Quintero Weaver, and Rodrigo and Fernando of Mapache Studies. I also want to send big abrazos out to my fellow AfroAmX comic book creators: Erika Alexander, Gil Ashby, Jiba Molei Anderson, Victor Dandridge, Eric Battle, Stanford Carpenter, Joe Robinson Currie, Mason Easley, Tim Fielder, Keith Knight, Dana McKnight, Arie Monroe, Bryan Christopher Moss, Ben Passmore, Uko Smith, Stacey Robinson, David Walker, Ron Wimberley, and Ashley A. Woods. Big props to my local Columbus comix crew, including J. M. Hunter, Dave Filipi, Jared Gardner, Jenny Robb, Caitlin McGurk, Jeff Smith, and Tom Spurgeon. I give a special shout-out to two compadre caped crusaders who always got my back, Christopher González and John Jennings.

I do this work for the next gen of Latinx, like my daughter, Corina Isabel, and her fellow '06 generation readers and creators. I take inspiration constantly from their superheroic capacity to overcome the seemingly insurmountable and their boundless creative talents that transform the infinitely imaginable into the playfully tangible. They are the future of creativity. They are *our* future.

Note: I use *Latinx* as well as *Latino/as* throughout the book. The frequent and strategic use of the LGBTQ inclusive Latinx signifier aims to remind readers of our community's rich and varied make up.

LATINX SUPERHEROES IN
MAINSTREAM COMICS

KICKING SOME *CULO*!

Whether good or evil, beautiful or ugly, smart or downright silly, able-bodied or differently abled, gay or straight, male or female, young or old, Latinx superheroes in mainstream comic book storyworlds (print comics, animation, TV, and film), DC and Marvel universes especially, are few and far between. I can count on one hand the number of Latinos in cartoons; on the other hand, I can count those in TV and film. Where we appear most is in print comics (DC and Marvel), but even here we number somewhere in the fifties—and this in a sea filled with hundreds of Anglo A- and B-listers.

Given the poor track records for representing people of color in comic book storyworlds, perhaps we shouldn't be surprised at this impoverished paucity. But we should be more than scratching our noggins. We should be upset. Indeed, if creators of superhero comic book storyworlds do as they *do*—to extrapolate, distill, then reconstruct from the building blocks that make up reality—then Latinos should be abundant. Yet we're not. We're 18-plus percent of the U.S. population, but we're barely a blip on the mainstream comic book storyworld radar. And within this demographic, we are Spanish speakers, Spanish and English speakers, English speakers, and of Cuban, Mexican, Dominican, Puerto Rican, Central American, and South American descent. This is to say, in addition to being the majority minority in the United States, Latinos are also very varied in their experience and identities. Latinoness, or Latinidad, varies from each subgroup that makes up the Latinx whole. Latino Puerto Rican culture in the United States is not identical to Puerto Rican island culture, nor is it identical to the culture of other U.S. Latinos of different origins. The comic book universe is only just beginning to clue in to this, and this after decades of being blind to Latinos as a whole in the United States.

Rather than focus on what's not present, this book is about throwing light on what (who) is. I mentioned already that it is within the print-comic realm that a majority of mainstream creations of Latino superheroes appear. Within this sliver of a much larger piece we see historically that most hail from the DC universe. Latinos begin to appear just after World War II with DC's Rodrigo "Rodney" Elwood Gaynor, followed by Santiago Vargas as El Gaucho in the 1950s. Rodney and El Gaucho were clean-cut and smart, and fought for the betterment of humanity. However, they were also light-skinned, criollo, landed gentry who chose to use their leisure time and vaquero skills to *save* their dark Latino indentured campesinos. While the Latino bandido character began to appear in the Marvel universe in the 1940s (the *Black Rider* series, for instance), when creators at Marvel finally did commit to making Latino superheroes, they were far more complex and rooted in their indigeneity. In the early 1970s, George Pérez introduced the comic book universe to the Nuyorican empowered White Tiger. And while late into the Latino superhero game Marvel quickly developed a more robust stable of complex Latino characters than did DC, it wasn't until the 1990s, when Anglo-Mexican Axel Alonso took over as editor in chief of DC, that we began to see more interesting Latino characterizations. (Axel would later step into the editor-in-chief shoes left behind by Joe Quesada at Marvel, who currently works as Marvel's chief creative officer.)

As I will begin to show by digging at and making visible a Latino superhero archive (print, animation, TV, and film), creations of such characters run the gamut from simple to complex in terms of plot, visual shaping, and characterization. Indeed, what I begin to show is how important not only the writing is in *making* Latino superheroes, but also the visual shaping. That some Latino superheroes soar and others belly-flop results from the degree of will to style present in the creative team's artistic (verbal, visual, and auditory) skill *and* responsibility to the subject matter. As I have discussed in my other work, the will to style is shorthand for identifying the responsibility of the creator (or creators) in understanding well the building blocks of reality that they are reconstructing as well as the degree of presence of a willful use of skills and technical devices to give shape to the making of new pop-cultural phenomena by and about Latinos. In the case of this book, we see that the more present the will to style, the more likely the Latino comic book superhero will *make* new our perception, thought, and feeling about real Latinos.

To create a sense of the flow from one slipstream (some wide and slow and others narrow and fast) into another, I divide the book into three main chapters, each with subsections. In chapter 1, "Excavating a Latinx Superhero Print-Comic Archive," I uncover, discover, and recover Latinx superheroes (and supervillains) that have come to populate the mainstream print comic book universe since the middle of the twentieth century. In building a historically chronological archive I begin to give shape to an understanding of how important both the visual and verbal elements are when making Latino protagonists. Those comic books that create compelling Latino characters are the ones that do their homework (that we take offense at being called Paco or that we don't all speak a truncated English with a heavily accented Spanish, for instance) and that skillfully and compellingly *geometrize* the visuals that make up their stories.

Here, too, I emphasize the fact that this archive or master narrative of Latinx superheroes in mainstream print comic book storyworlds doesn't necessarily follow a trajectory of improvement. Just as we saw a diminished will to *geometrize* and *storyfy* Latinos in the 1950s, so, too, do we see some of this continue today. Some push the envelope of creativity, while others lazily repeat the stereotypical and familiar. The archive I recover, then, is not one of a *natural* progression toward a more careful and complete (in matters of form and content) creation of Latinos in comic book storyworlds.

In chapter 2, "*Toward* a Theory of Latinx Comic Book Superheroes," I consider the mental processes involved in the reader/viewer's co-creation of Latino superheroes. I don't consider our engagement with these comics as passive; hence, the emphasis on our role as *co-creators* of these storyworlds. I then begin to theorize the huge importance of the visuals in shaping superhero comic book stories; this is less the case in the alternative comic book storytelling modes. I then begin to theorize the importance of the verbal elements in shaping these comic book storyworlds. A comic book can give complex, kinetic shape to Latino superheroes, but if the writing is weak, the comic falls flat.

In chapter 3, "Multimediated Latinx Superheroes," I begin to excavate the archive of Latinos in mainstream animation, TV, and film. I recover a handful of Latino superheroes. I discover a whole lot more Latinx superhero erasures. Here again, I discuss the importance of the presence of a willfulness on the part of the creators, both in terms of making complex Latino superheroes *and* in terms of willfully erasing them from the multiple media(ted) comic book landscape. With the *X-Men* and *Batman* re-creations, for example, we see that Latino superheroes created in the original print comics never make it onto pixelated, TV, or silver screens. I also discuss how Latinos end up on the postproduction room floors, such as in the making of Kenneth Branagh's *Thor* (2011). I discuss, too, how we aren't even present in contemporary set superhero films that reflect more accurately (and convincingly to audiences) urban landscapes that are increasingly Latino. In the two-hour-plus runtime of Zack Snyder's *Superman: Man of Steel* (2013), only two Latinos appear: a gas station attendant and an infantry soldier. In his *Batman v. Superman* (2016), with its even longer (and more exhausting) runtime, Latinos appear, but south of the U.S.-Mexico border and in Day of the Dead regalia. One way or another, in animation, TV, and film, Latinos are being actively disappeared.

Latinx Superheroes in Mainstream Comics is about throwing open some doors and windows. It's about excavating a living, breathing archive. It's the beginning of an articulation of *how* creators (authors, artists, animators, and directors) use a whole variety of shaping devices to make (and erase) Latinx superheroes in comic book storyworlds. In the end, this book is a journey into how some Latinx superheroes kick *culo* and soar to unimagined heights because of the careful and *willful* use of formal devices and creating of compelling content that *makes new* our perception, thought, and feeling about the world Latinos exist within and superheroically transform.

Chapter 1

EXCAVATING A LATINX SUPERHERO PRINT-COMIC ARCHIVE

Alpha to Omega: Latinos in the Comic Book Slipstream

Comic book histories have done a lousy job of documenting the presence of Latino superheroes. Take a look at the more recent DK tomes like *The Marvel Encyclopedia: Updated and Expanded* (2014) and *The DC Encyclopedia* (2016). They mention only a few of the many Latino superheroes and supervillains that have shaped the Marvel and DC universes. And while African American and gay superheroes are mentioned breezily in documentaries such as PBS's *Superheroes: A Never-Ending Battle* (October 15, 2013) and the History Channel's *Comic Book Superheroes Unmasked* (2003), Latinos are conspicuously absent from these apparent histories.

While clearly not legion (around fifty by my count), Latino superheroes have been and continue to be present in mainstream in-print comics. They have played and continue to play a significant role in shaping the mainstream comic book superhero universe—and multiverse. Indeed, creators of mainstream comics have had Latino superheroes on the radar since the 1940s. It's been increasingly the case of late.

At the outset here I offer an initial typology of Latino superheroes, something that we will see fleshed out as the book unfolds. Whereas Anglo superheroes (often characterized as recast Manifest Destiny cowboy types injected with invincibility) tend to defend the nation but are somehow apart from it, Latino superheroes tend to be linked to the community. Bonita Juarez as Firebird takes down threats to the national order and is a community social worker by day. Unlike their Anglo peers, Latino superheroes in the mainstream have tended to be identified more with their bodies and emotions (usually raw and out of control) than minds. Anglo superheroes tend to be identified either as already born special or within an entitled, meritocratic-rise-to-omnipotence prototype narrative; Latino superheroes are more likely to follow a bildungs-roman prototype narrative, having to *learn* to become and *work at* becoming superheroes. Anglo superheroes sport outfits that act as stand-ins for their powers. Latino superheroes tend to accessorize in ways that root them in pre-Columbian histories and the Latino community. Latino creator Edgardo Miranda-Rodríguez outfits his Latina superhero, La Borinqueña, in a costume with the colors of the Puerto Rican flag. He invests her with powers that spring from her contemporary experiences and identity as a Puerto Rican (Boricua) that grows from her native Taino ancestry. He also invests her with personality traits and superpowers "that make her fully Boricua: love of family, patience and selflessness" (16), Miranda-Rodríguez tells Monica Rohr in an interview. Unlike their Anglo peers, Latino superheroes tend to experience a different set of struggles with their dual identities: civilian ordinary and superhero secret, but as cast within proximate and extended family kinship structures, working-class communities, and a strong presence of Catholicism (and its syncretic variants such as Santeria). Of course, as this book will begin to demonstrate, Latino superheroes present all variation of the above types, and much more. And this becomes increasingly the case as we move from their incipient appearance in the 1940s to the renaissance that takes place as we move into the twenty-first century.

That today's mainstream comic book storyworlds have more Latinos/as than earlier epochs is not surprising. Latinos have become the largest minority group in the United States, increasingly outnumbering the Anglo majority in more and more regions. And with this increasing majority presence we have also seen the rise of Latinos as consumers *and* creators. (See the appendix for a partial list of Latino and Latin American creators working for DC and Marvel.) With such a Latino reality pushing up against the doors of the mainstream in-print comic book marketplace, it's become harder to deny our presence in superhero storyworlds.

Of course, demographic shifts alone do not ensure increased presence in mainstream popular culture. However, what is a fact is that it becomes harder—and arguably more shameful—when industry behemoths like DC and Marvel ignore this reality. While it's likely a dollar-profit that's motivating DC and Marvel to create more Latino superheroes of late, the upshot has been a veritable uptick in their creation. DC's New 52 reboots, such as *Justice League, Justice League of America, Nova,* and *Vibe,* for instance, all feature Latinx superheroes. And there are Marvel's recent runs with Anya Ayala as Spider-Girl, Robbie Reyes as the new Ghost Rider, and Miles Morales as the Blatino Spider-Man.

But to get here (the present), we have to return to there (the past). Turning the clock back to sleuth out the *few* Latinos who appeared before and even during the Bronze Age (1970–1985) era of comics means performing some superheroic scholarly acrobatics of my own: to bend and twist like Plastic Man (DC) in all directions; to channel the strength of The Thing (Marvel) to turn over any and every block; to penetrate beneath surfaces with interpretive X-ray vision; to use psionic forces to pull to the surface traces of brownness (Latinoness) beneath white surfaces. Always with an eye out for Latinos in the DC and Marvel universes, I've amassed a private archive of mainstream comics that feature Latinos/as. Fortunately, too, DC and Marvel have their own fan-based databases that allowed me to cross-reference and verify these Latinx superheroes and many others. (For DC visit http://dc.wikia.com/wiki/DC_Comics_Database, and for Marvel visit http://marvel.wikia.com/wiki/Marvel_Database.)

Different superpowered psychological and physical enhancements are useful for different parts of this scholarly excavation. For instance, an optically enhanced vision penetrates the surface of Krypton's Vathlo Island to reveal how its ethnic-looking inhabitants are stand-ins for Latinos (*Superman* #238, 1971). The skillful manipulation of a critical-race-theory superpower allows me to formulate a critique about how Lois Lane's adoption of an orphaned Native American girl uncritically repeats the United States' history of "adopting" out (kidnapping) indigenous children as a form of forceful assimilation.

Outer galactic forged helmets help transport me across time and space to 1947, to issue 77 of *Master Comics* that features a nine-page story ("The Border Incident") that follows the telepathic, circus-raised, radar-visioning Pep Pepper as Radar the International Policeman. In "The Border Incident" we follow Radar as he travels to "Rolivia" and "Teru." He's on a crusade to bring equality and justice to oppressed subjects of the Third World, bringing his capitalist ideology and beneficent father-as-savior attitude to free the helpless "natives"—and to liberate the Third World generally.

Figure 3. Superman's Girl Friend Lois Lane, "Indian Death Charge," #110 (May 1971).

Certainly, making visible the Latino presence in the DC and Marvel worlds does require activation of superheroic powers. With these superpowers in play we soon discover that Latinos do appear throughout comic book history. They appear in various shades, shapes, sizes, smarts, and derring-dos. They appear with greater and lesser degrees of visual and verbal presence. As I'll begin to show below, each comic book creation demonstrates a different degree of a willful use of teams of creators' mental mechanisms and technical know-how. That is, they do a good *and* bad job at distilling and reconstructing Latinx identities and experiences.

First Encounters . . . of the Criollo Kind

In 1940, All-American Publications (now DC) introduced issue 1 of *Flash Comics*, and with it the first positively identified Latino "superhero" to appear in mainstream comics. John Wentworth (author) and George Storm (artist) created Rodrigo "Rodney" Elwood Gaynor as The Whip. Like Zorro, he's light-skinned and wealthy; he's a former polo champion. And while he's not of European birth (like Zorro), he's still light-skinned. That is, his social status and skin color clearly identify him as *not* of the Mexican farming working class, but as criollo (of Spanish descent). He takes on the savior role after a chance encounter with Carlos, a Mexican farmer about to be lynched. Wentworth and Storm characterize The Whip as a vigilante who defends the rights of the exploited—the poor and naïve Mexicans of the fictional town Seguro.

All-American Publications did introduce a smart, urban identified Latino during this early period of comics, the super smart orphan Anthony Rodriguez of New York's Suicide Slum in Joe Simon and Jack Kirby's *Star-Spangled Comics* (vol. 1, #7, April 1942). While there's not much in his characterization (neither in backstory nor in other physical attributes) to identify him as Latino, Joe Simon does invest this urban-dwelling Latino with a prodigious vocabulary. He's known as "Big Words"—a superpower of sorts as he's the only one of the ragtag orphan team known as the Newsboy Legion who can understand some of the ways adults speak.

Unfortunately, Simon and Kirby's characterization of a Latino as smart and urban was not the path followed by others. For instance, in 1949 Bill Finger (writer) and David V. Reed (artist) introduce something of the opposite: a Latino sociopathic supervillain known as El Papagayo (*Batman*, "Ride, Bat-Hombre, Ride," #56). While Finger and Reed put some geographic distance between U.S. readers and this Latino supervillain, he's still characterized as sociopathic. They locate El Papagayo in an unnamed South American space. That is, they situate this re-creation of Latinoness at a safe distance. And they exoticize him. He comes with an exotic parrot, Toto, also characterized as sociopathic. In later incarnations, El Papagayo moves closer to home. Michael Fleisher (writer) and José Luis García-López (artist) transplant him

Figure 4. El Papagayo in *Batman*, "Ride, Bat-Hombre, Ride," #56 (December 1, 1949).

to the U.S. Southwest in the *Jonah Hex* series, for instance (*Jonah Hex*, "Carlota Conspiracy," #9, February 1978).

The Latino as sociopath had a greater hold in the industry than do-gooders like The Whip. While The Whip does reappear in other series, he never quite gets the same attention or momentum as El Papagayo, who is endlessly resurrected over long stretches of time. As recently as 2010, El Papagayo appears, and this time in the post-crisis New Earth universe of *Batman Incorporated* (2010–) created by Grant Morrison (writer) as well as Yanick Paquette and Pere Pérez (artists). The creators identify El Papagayo as an Argentinean with sociopathic tendencies and as a formidable member of the Club of Villains, which includes Latinos: the *luchador* El Sombrero and the supervillainess Scorpiana.

Figure 5. El Papagayo II in *Batman Incorporated* #3 (March 2011).

South America becomes a "safe" space for the construction not only of supervillain Latinos, but also of good-guy sidekicks. For instance, with the arrival of an Argentine-based Batman in the 1950s we see the making of the criollo crusader, Santiago Vargas as El Gaucho (*Detective Comics* #215, January 1955)—a term used in Argentina and Uruguay to identify nineteenth-century cowboys who freely roamed the Argentine pampas; they also wore a sash (faja) around the waist and used *boleadoras* (strips of leather with stones on the end) to herd and catch cattle. Indeed, we begin to see the creation of a Latino character where his author (Edmond Hamilton) and artist (Sheldon Moldoff) start to exercise a modicum of a will to style when it comes to characterization. He's another masked, well-heeled criollo (think The Whip), but at least his outfit has something to do with the Argentine gaucho sartorial tradition. In addition to his faja, he wields a boleadora. Unlike his predecessors, too, he gets down and dirty when he defends the poor, fighting also with his fists.

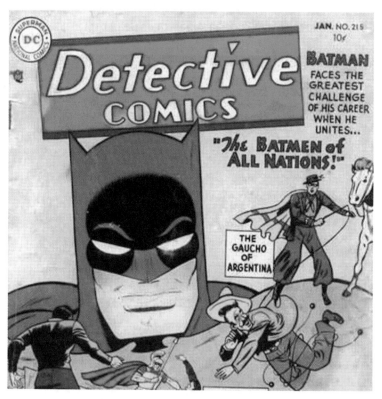

Figure 6. El Gaucho in *Detective Comics* #215 (January 1955).

This said, the rest of El Gaucho's characterization continues to solidify that white-savior narrative to poor, unthinking "brown" Latinos. There's never a moment in his story arc when we see the uneducated brown folk organizing and revolting against their exploiters. They always need leadership of a criollo savior. In other incarnations he becomes phenotypically darker, goateed, with a black leather jacket and a red bandana, and characterized as more macho. For instance, when he appears in *Wonder Woman*, vol. 1, #263 (January 1980), the cover headlines: "Even with all her powers Wonder Woman is no match for the Gaucho—a real man!" And, when El Gaucho appears in *Batman Incorporated* (2010–2011; collected in vol. 1 in 2013), he sports a leather jacket but sheds the green pantaloons, and his red bandana acts more like a *luchador-*style mask. His goatee morphs into a handlebar mustache. The only symbol of his gauchismo is his continued use of the *boleadora*. He's a macho Latino savior with a rough-and-tumble street makeover. Most radically, Morrison characterizes him as a Spanish speaker (even though we read his words in English)—a feature neglected by Hamilton in the earlier 1950s iteration. And, unlike earlier iterations, language becomes a marker of pro- or antinationalist sentiment. That he refuses to speak English is identified as an anti-imperialist maneuver.

Figure 7. El Gaucho of Earth-1 in *Wonder Woman*, #263 (January 1980).

Figure 8. El Gaucho in *Batman Incorporated*, vol. 1 (2013).

The twenty-first-century makeover of El Gaucho appears progressive—he's street and anti-imperialist. Along with others featured in *Batman Inc.*, such as Man-of-Bats and Raven, El Gaucho becomes a figure who, as Katharina Bieloch and Sharif Bitar remark, "decenters the American icon—Batman—to show that crossing into other national, cultural traditions transnationalizes the superhero figure as well as transforms our sense of the U.S. as exceptional" ("Batman Goes Transnational: The Global Appropriation and Distribution of an American Hero," 114). Indeed, at one moment Raven mentions the high unemployment, teenage suicide, and lack of infrastructure that create wastelands of Native American reservations. With Morrison at the helm, a character like El Gaucho and other marginalized identity superheroes actively remind readers that the United States is imploding with its own internalized colonial and imperialist agenda. (See *Transnational Perspectives on Global Narratives: Comics at the Crossroads*. Eds. Shane Denson, Christina Meyer, and Daniel Stein. London. New York: Bloomsbury Academic, 2013, 13–26.) But, of course, this is the twenty-first century. I'm getting ahead of this story and myself.

As we move through the history of the creation of Latino superheroes and supervillains in DC and Marvel in-print comics, we begin to see not only more Latino characters with more or less greater complexity in their characterization, but also the growth of a more capacious set of devices that give visual shape to the characters. Indeed, as we move into the next decades and finally into the twenty-first century, we also move from the use of four-color clusters to digital technologies. This has given creators a more abundant set of devices for visually giving shape to Latino superheroes and supervillains. That is, as time passes and drawing technologies proliferate, we see greater possibilities for creators to *geometrize* Latino storyworlds: from the staid color scheme and panel layout seen in The Whip to the kinetic and dynamic storytelling of Morrison and Paquette.

This said, just because there have been advances in technologies for visually shaping Latino comic book storyworlds doesn't mean that the industry has necessarily been advancing toward the complex in the representation of Latinos. Indeed, there are plenty of DC and Marvel comics made today that fall as flat as stories seen with The Whip.

Brown Tints to Silver and Bronze

As we move from the late Golden Age into the latter part of the Silver Age of comics and into the Bronze Age (approximately 1970 to 1985), we see the arrival of more Latino superheroes and supervillains. Indeed, as Marco Arnaudo discusses generally of this period, we see more interest in creating superheroes from the racial and ethnic margins. For Arnaudo, the multicultural cast of X-Men who appear in 1975 marks this move to present a panoply of multiethnic superheroes with a variety of methods and approaches to heal a social tissue that's been ripped apart. These multiethnic superheroes do not seek to defend, according to Arnaudo, "the status quo but rather the conditions of freedom that allow citizens to decide for themselves whether to maintain that status quo or whether and in what way to change it" (*The Myth of the Superhero*, 111). And, in *Death, Disability, and the Superhero*, José Alaniz speaks of this Silver Age moment in mainstream comics as a kind of renaissance for race, gender, sexuality, and disability superheroes. Moreover, for Alaniz, these superheroes use their ethnoracial, sexual, and differently abled subjectivities as sources of super empowerment. For the first time, we see those traditionally swept to the margins affirmed—and empowered by their difference. The Silver Age begins to move multiethnic superheroes from the shadows into the limelight, and with this we also see the fleshing out of character and geometrizing of narrative art of superheroes rooted in their struggles as the disenfranchised.

The most significant creator during this period was the Latino George Pérez. In 1975, along with Bill Mantlo (writer), Pérez created one of the most compelling Latino superheroes to date: the Nuyorican Hector Ayala as White Tiger. With Pérez and Mantlo's introduction of White Tiger in *Deadly Hands of Kung Fu* #19 (December 1975) we see for the first time in comic books a masterful creation of a fully realized Latino superhero. This happens not only because of a responsibility to the verbal content (Mantlo did his homework when it came to re-creating bilingual expression, for instance) but also in Pérez's masterful geometrizing of Ayala's character:

Figure 9. White Tiger in *Deadly Hands of Kung Fu*, "The Beginning," #20 (January 1976).

with his hair and facial features Pérez anchors his contemporary urban Nuyorican-ness in Afrolatino ancestry. He's a proud Nuyorican; one of the T-shirts he wears reads "Puerto Rico We Down." He's bilingual. He's smart (attends Empire State University). He's expressive. He's dynamic.

Without the condescension or outsiderness seen in earlier Latino creations, here Pérez and Mantlo create a contemporary, urban, linguistically and ancestrally rooted Latino; the solid, triangular stance shown in the first panel above emphasizes this firm rootedness. When he transforms into White Tiger, we really see Pérez's will to geometrize the story at work: the black-and-white backdrop as negative space surrounds an oversize ferocious tiger's head to emphasize its power. Pérez's geometry then works to dynamically push Ayala's transformation into White Tiger to the foreground. The placement of the word balloons creates moments of affective congruence between the kinetic effect of the geometry and the sound we hear in our minds when we follow the speech bubbles down, then across the page to the crescendo: "But I know that I'm . . . The White Tiger."

Indeed, Pérez and Mantlo's careful attention to both Ayala's

Figure 10. White Tiger in *Deadly Hands of Kung Fu* #19 (December 1975).

verbal and visual characterization infuses his character with a substance and dynamism not seen in mainstream comics. They choose to create a superhero with his identity firmly planted in his Latinidad; and, with this, a powerful drive to protect his community against menacing underworld oppressors, Latino and otherwise. In *Deadly Hands of Kung Fu* #19, there's a scene in the rail yards where Pérez portrays him discovering his super speed and martial arts agility, taking out a couple of white street thugs who have just beaten up a security guard. Pérez's geometrizing of the story draws our attention forcefully to his actions: we feel the movement of his body, the intensity of his emotions (even behind a mask), and the force of his exhortations. This richness of visual and verbal storytelling comes together in the creating of Ayala. Unlike those that had come before that we read and forget (or read only for scholarly historical purposes), here we want to go back again and again to relish in verbal and visual construction this Latino superhero. They lift the bar high for others to step up and accept the challenge in using verbal and visual means to create a compelling Latino superhero. (Decades later, in *Daredevil II* #40 [February 2003], Brian Michael Bendis [writer] and Terry and Rachel Dodson [artists] finally bring Ayala's story arc to a close when he's shot dead by police.)

With the gauntlet thrown down, other creative teams either stepped to the Pérez/Mantlo challenge, or didn't. For instance, in 1977, E. Nelson Bridwell (writer) and Ramona Fradon (artist) choose also to create an urban-based Latino character: Bernal Rojas as Bushmaster (*The Super Friends*, "The Mind Killers," #8, November 1977). While his name and day job (herpetologist) might suggest that Rojas is an exotic, tropical-based Latino character, they give him an urban identity: he's from Caracas, Venezuela. Of course, Bridwell and Fradon are not only picking up the baton from Pérez/Mantlo in making an urban Latino character, but also doing a modicum of work to reconstruct their contemporary reality: the beginnings of a shift from rural to urban Latino populations. And while they choose to visually characterize him as hypercorporeal (he's big and muscled), they also choose to characterize him as rational, educated (he studies amphibians and reptiles), and bilingual; Bridwell and Fradon use the convention of the angle brackets < > to indicate that he's speaking Spanish. And he's deeply rooted in his South American heritage in a new and novel way. He uses his smarts to create a high-tech suit that allows him to transmogrify into any South American reptile. That is, he is a Latino, characterized by his bodily presence *and* literally in a reptilian way, but he's also smart and rational in all that he does. A decade-plus later, Paul Kupperberg (writer) and Dan Rodriguez's (artist) *Justice League Quarterly* ("The Heart of Darkness," #17, 1994) brings Bushmaster into the Global Guardians fold when he joins this worldly team of superheroes, which includes Beatriz "Bea" Bonilla da Costa as Green Fury (also known as Green Flame)—the first Latina superhero created in the mainstream comic book universe.

Figure 11. Green Fury (or Fire) in *Justice League of America*, vol. 1, #102 (August 1995).

In October 1979, E. Nelson Bridwell (writer) and Ramona Fradon (artist) introduce Green Fury (*The Super Friends* #25). Bridwell chooses to characterize her as of Brazilian ancestry; she's the arch-protector of Brazil. Fradon (penciler) and Gene D'Angelo (colorist) choose to portray Green Fury as more of Euro-Spanish descent than Afrolatino: she's light-skinned, with Caucasian facial features. That said, they do create her as a polyglot (Spanish, Portuguese, and English) and give her powers that vanquish villains, and also heal. As she evolves in the DC universe, however, she's depicted as in need of Anglo A-listers to save the day *and* increasingly sexualized. On the cover of *The Super Friends* #47 (August 1, 1981) she thinks to herself: "Can't defeat them all! If only the Super Friends were here to help me." In other iterations, Green Fury (also known as Fire and Green Flame) is portrayed as hyper-corporeal, the object of the straight male gaze as either Brazilian lingerie model, showgirl, or stage performer. As her superhero identity evolves, her costume seems to get skimpier. We see this in *Justice League of America*, vol. 1, #102 (August 1995), when artists Chuck Wojtkiewicz, Bob Dvorak, and Gene D'Angelo portray her welcoming of Icemaiden to the Global Guardians.

By the time 2003 rolls around, Green Fury completely loses her clothes. On the cover of *Formerly Known as the Justice League*, vol. 1, #4 (December 2003), writers Keith Giffen and J. M. DeMatteis, along with artists Kevin Maguire and Joe Rubinstein, choose to portray a multitude of male superheroes gawking at her and variously commenting: "Hey, look! It's a girl!" "Yeah, but she's on fire." "Who cares? It's a girl!"

In *Justice League: Generation Lost* (2010), visual creative team Aaron Lopresti and Matt Ryan geometrize Green Fury's physicality in ways that plump up her lips, narrow her waist, and accentuate her breasts. With Green Fury (or Fire or Green Flame) we see the beginning of a trend to geometrize Latina superheroes as hyper-sexualized objects.

When it comes to the trend to characterize Latino superheroes as urban, Bill Mantlo (writer) and Sal Buscema's (artist) creation of Bonita Juarez as Firebird is an exception. In their 1981 intro-duction of Firebird they choose to root her character in rural New Mexico (*The Incredible Hulk*, vol. 1, #265). While certainly outside the trend to urbanize Latino superheroes and to portray them as phenotypically more Anglo-looking than mestiza (of indigenous and European descent), Mantlo does invest her with smarts and a strong sense of community activism. She's a social worker by day. And for the first time we see the making of a Latina superhero who struggles with her Latinidad. She struggles with reconciling the ecstasy she experiences with her godlike superhero powers of flight and fire with her Catholicism. After struggling with the idea that her superpowers might be the work of the devil ("I almost confessed to Father Ramirez!"), she comes to understand that she can use them as "a force for good." There's a great will to style both in the writing and visuals with the making of Firebird that makes this Latina superhero psychologically complex and physically kinetic. Unfortunately, however, she never attains the same level of respect as her Anglo peers. For instance, in a non-self-conscious manner Mantlo and Buscema wrap up issue 265 with Firebird and Native American Red Wolf doing all the work to save the people from Hulk, but with Anglo superheroes Texas Twister (who calls Firebird "Mex-Chick") and Shooting Star arriving on the scene just in time to take all the glory.

Figure 12. Green Fury on the cover of *Formerly Known as the Justice League*, vol. 1, #4 (December 2003).

As seen in so much of U.S. history (cultural, social, and polit-ical), indigenous and Latino peoples (as represented by Red Wolf and Firebird) do the work but receive none of the recognition. Unfortunately, without self-awareness of this built into the comic, it simply reproduces uncritically this narrative and historical trend.

After the appearance of Firebird we see far fewer rural-based Latinos created in mainstream comics. Even those set in South America take place in urban settings. And with this urbanization we also see a greater set of struggles presented: from racism to sexism, homophobia, and able-bodied privilege.

In 1982, Chris Claremont (writer) and Bob McLeod (artist) introduce to the Marvel universe Roberto "Bobby" da Costa as Sunspot (*Marvel Graphic Novel* #4, September 7, 1982). Both in the writing and the visuals of Claremont, McLeod (drawing and inking), and Glynis Wein (color) we see a will to style that locates him in his Afro-Brazilian Latinidad: he's born and raised in Rio de Janeiro (then later in Harlem), has dark skin and black curly hair, and is anchored in an important Latino tradition, playing *fútbol*. And while he's identified as of-body (soccer player), Claremont invests him with some serious smarts. He's second-generation college-educated (his mama's an archaeologist) and polylingual (Portuguese, English, Chinese, Askani, and Spanish).

Figure 13. Introduction of Bobby in *Marvel Graphic Novel*, vol. 1, #4 (September 7, 1982).

Figure 14. Bobby is beaten up by a white player in *Marvel Graphic Novel*, vol. 1, #4 (September 7, 1982).

Figure 15. Bobby transforms into Sunspot in *Marvel Graphic Novel*, vol. 1, #4 (September 7, 1982).

Figure 16. Bobby uses superpowers to fight a white
soccer player in *Marvel Graphic Novel*, vol. 1, #4
(September 7, 1982).

Claremont introduces an important new ingredient to the
characterization of Latino superheroes: racism. On the field Bobby
takes a beating by a racist member of the opposing team, the
Dynamos. This triggers the manifesting of a metahuman gene. He
transforms into black solar energy. In addition to this being identified as his mutant superpower, with McLeod (inker) and Wein
(color) making his solar energy *black* (and not orange, red, or yel-
low, for instance), they guide our meaning-making processes to
understand this as his transformation into something painful but
also as his embrace and affirmation of his racial, black Afrolatino
identity. So, while he's a Latino who gets angry and turns into this
black solar energy entity, it's not without justification; he responds
to a racist world. He's not *hot-tempered* in that stereotypical,
fly-off-the-handle way we see so often in the representation of
Latinos. And this because McLeod is careful to contextualize his
anger: he's a young, dark Afrolatino growing up in a xenophobic
world. And his acute sense of his racialized identity later manifests

itself when, after being made to feel a second-class citizen to the Anglo mutant A-listers at Professor X's academy, he decides to join Magneto's antiheroic mutant team, who are more accepting of him and other racially Othered mutants.

While, generally speaking, the trend in mainstream comics during the 1980s was to begin to ground Latino superheroes in specifics of place and time that relate to the different struggles and experiences (racism or otherwise) within the Latino community, there are still comic book creations out of time and place. Claremont and Buscema's creation of Amara Aquilla as Magma (and one of Sunspot's love-obsessions) is a case in point. In October 1983, they introduce her in *New Mutants*, "The Road to . . . Rome" (#8). She's a Latina from Brazil. However, it's a Brazil out of time and place: Nova Roma, deep in the Amazon jungle, where she and her tribe are completely cut off from the rest of the world. Her mutant power is more exotic than connected to some real-world struggle: she can create earthquakes by shifting tectonic plates and fire magma from her body. Arguably her best feature: smart-ass sass.

With the exception of Amara, the trend was to urbanize—and complicate—Latino superheroes. And while Gerry Conway (writer) and Chuck Patton (artist) create the urban-dwelling (Detroit) in Francisco "Paco" Ramon as Vibe, they miss the mark on complicating his identity. This includes the careless and offensive "Paco" (akin to calling a white character something like Cracker) and the lazy and stereotypical portrayal of Vibe as the former leader of the gang Los Lobos. And when Vibe speaks he does so with truncated, phonetically odd-sounding English phrases such as "wachu gonna do." Artist Chuck Patton chooses to visually portray Vibe with chisel-jawed, more Anglo facial features than those we might recognize as mestizo. His powers: psionic vibratory power and break-dance moves. Conway and Patton create a Latino superhero who is all stereotype: *all* body and no brain. (George Pérez was so offended that, when asked to draw Vibe for *JLA/Avengers*, he couldn't bear to draw all of him, showing only fragments of him in any given panel. See his *Focus on George Pérez*.) On one occasion, Vibe uses break-dance moves and metahuman vibratory powers to defeat the African American supervillain Crowbar, who is also *all* body and no brain (*Justice League of America*, vol. 1, #233). Careless portrayals of racialized subjects along with the Latinos vs.

African Americans story line do little to destabilize destructive and racist denigrative representations of the ethnoracial Other in the United States.

Figure 17. Paco Ramon as Vibe, introduced in *Justice League of America*, "Rebirth One," #233 (December 1984).

In October 1986, Roy Thomas (writer) and Todd McFarlane (artist) introduce to the Infinity Inc. team the Latina Yolanda Martinez as Wildcat II; she's the goddaughter of Anglo superhero Ted Grant as Wildcat from the 1940s. Ted Grant's compadre was Yolanda's father, "Mauler" Montez. Within the bigger DC universe, Yolanda is also the cousin of Alex Montez. (I also discuss Alex later in this chapter.) With Grant paralyzed, Yolanda decides to come out of the closet as a genetically modified metahuman and continue Montez's vigilante work as the Latina-identified "new Wildcat!!!" (*Crisis on Infinite Earths*, #6, September 1986). The DC creators portray Yolanda Martinez as bilingual, urban (Gotham), and educated. She's a journalist by trade. And while DC's creative team focuses on Wildcat's physicality—the geometrizing of her body as accentuated hip and breast curves—and not on her brain (her journalistic pen), she's given a phenotypic shading of brown and agency not seen with Green Fury. (Notably, in the late 1990s Wildcat once again traverses gender but remains Latino when

Hector Ramirez takes on the mantle, fighting crime in Gotham till his untimely death at the hands of Killer Croc in *Batman/Wildcat* #1, April 1997.)

With greater attention paid to issues of race and gender in the DC and Marvel universes, we also see a turn to struggles of disability as it intersects with Latino identity and experience. In 1987, Marv Wolfman (writer) and Jerry Ordway (artist) introduce a barrio-grown-and-educated Latino, Jose Delgado as Gangbuster (*Adventures of Superman* #428, May 1987). Wolfman identifies him as a high school teacher living in Metropolis's Suicide Slum. And, unlike many of the other Latino superheroes discussed so far, he was not born with superpowers. He trains himself to become an expert boxer and martial arts fighter, with a special skill in wielding nunchucks. With his protective gear and self-taught warrior skills he sets out to protect Metropolis's citizens, battling all variety of urban thugs and organized gangs. In a battle with Combattor to save Lois Lane, he ends up paralyzed from the waist down; he regains his ability to walk (LexCorp implants), but temporarily loses total self-control. Lex Luthor uses the implants to control Gangbuster, manipulating him to fight Superman. DC invests Gangbuster with tremendous complexity. He walks *and* fights again, but aided by corporate-designed (and controlled) cybernetic technology. The able-bodied enhancements give him the use of his legs and superpowered physical strength, but put into question his freedom to choose what actions he wants to take to transform the world. Moreover, Wolfman never loses sight of everyday concerns for differently abled, racialized subjects: as a differently abled Latino, Delgado struggles to find employment.

In the late 1980s, DC put sexuality front and center. Steve Englehart (writer) and Joe Staton (artist) introduce the first gay Latino superhero, Gregorio de la Vega as Extraño. He is of Peruvian descent and a member of a global team of international superheroes who make up the New Guardians, also known as the Chosen (*Millennium*, vol. 1, #1, January 1988). While Richard T. Rodríguez points out that the creation of Extraño was important for gay readers of the comics, they were also disturbed, especially by the unrealistic way that he's killed off by contracting HIV from the supervillain Hemo-Goblin. Englehart and Staton certainly demonstrate a poor will to style, slipping into careless gay stereotypes. Englehart has Extraño speak in an excessively flamboyant manner ("Puh-lease!). Staton visualizes him with a pencil mustachio, pinched-up face, and flamboyant, emasculating gestures and body poses. He's more interested in coordinating sartorial wear than battling the universe's supervillains. This said, his appearance, as Rodriguez reminds us, "generated urgent critical debates regarding issues concerning race, sexuality, and HIV/AIDS" ("Revealing Secret Identities," 227).

Figure 18. Wildcat goes mano a mano with her Spanish-speaking cousin, the human/shark hybrid villain Carcharo in *Infinity Inc.*, vol. 1, #25 (April 1986).

Figure 19. Gregorio de la Vega as Extraño in *Millenium*, vol. 1, #1 (January 1988).

In 1989, Gerard Jones (writer) and Mike Parobeck (artist) give a Latino makeover to the original Anglo Lazarus Lane as El Diablo with the introduction of Rafael Sandoval (*El Diablo*, vol. 2, #1, August 1989). In the original version, Lane is revived by a Native American shaman, Wise Owl, and becomes a Zorro-like vigilante figure. In his Latino iteration he is an urban-grown Latino, educated (city council member) and physically fit (trained boxer), who decides to don the El Diablo outfit to bring a vigilante-style justice to criminals hounding the citizens of the Southwest in the borderland city of Dos Rios. While Jones gives the new El Diablo an interesting set of motivations and action—ridding the barrio of drugs and gangs—Jones doesn't do much more to add to what we've already seen with Latino superheroes. In fact, both Jones and Parobeck slip into careless stereotypes, not in terms of sexual identity, but in terms of language and costume, dialogue and visuals: the character speaks an odd phonetic English (peppered with some Spanglish); in terms of lines, layout, and coloring, he's drawn with angular, static shapes and lines that accentuate chiseled features one might expect to see in an Anglo Batman; his disguise is drawn in red, black, and white; his torero suit and mask flatten more than intensify interest in his character. Stereotypes and lackluster issues aside, Jones does write some interesting, even revelatory moments into the story. For instance, as city council representative, Sandoval meets with community organizers to discuss the issue of drugs and violence in the barrio (*El Diablo*, vol. 1, #1,

August 1989). He tells one of the organizers, Olga Zamora, that the protection of the community needs to come from the people themselves. Olga responds, "I'm all in favor of grassroots groups, Mr. Sandoval . . . But the people of El Barrio need some assurance that the city government cares whether their children live or die . . . Something more than words" (4). That is, Sandoval advocates for a community-based-and-supported vigilantism, foreshadowing much of what is happening in places like Mexico today, where the police no longer protect the people; where the police are as corrupt as the cartels they protect. Pushed into a corner, the community seeks to take justice in their own hands but doesn't entirely exonerate the state from doing the job of protecting its citizens. Jones gets at the heart of problems Latinos face in communities where gangs are the law of the land. Yet when it comes to the writing of the character, El Diablo, he relies on clichés and stereotypes.

In September 2008, Jai Nitz (writer), along with Phil Hester and Ande Parks (artists), resurrects El Diablo as the gangster thug Chato Santana in the six-issue *El Diablo*, vol. 3 series. They create him as a true borderland subject: "I was born in L.A., but I grew up in Mexico. I was the only U.S. citizen in my family." A Latino gang-banger shot and paralyzed by an Anglo drug enforcement agent ("DOJ"), Chato signs a deal with Lazarus Lane to become hell's new assassin. He transforms into the immortal superhero with supernatural blazing-fire whip riding a blazing-fire-eyed black stallion (*El Diablo*, vol. 3, #1, November 2008). Hester and Parks visualize him not as a staid and static Latino do-gooder with a stereotypical torero outfit as seen with Mike Parobeck's 1989 abovementioned characterization, but as a dynamic *luchador*-style superhero cowboy who rides a red-eyed, wild black stallion. Chato accepts his new role and destiny, and "the curse that would compel me to punish the wicked. To punish men like me" (*El Diablo*, vol. 3, #6, April 2009). That is, Nitz creates Chato as the cursed new El Diablo who seeks redemption by destroying the wicked. He determines who lives and who dies. Notably, too, El Diablo resurfaces yet again in 2011, when Adam Glass (writer) and Federico Dalloccohio (artist) bring him back into the DC fold as a key member of the newly formed Suicide Squad—a multiethnic bad-guy team that includes African American Black Spider, Asian American Yo-Yo, and the hybrid man-shark, King Shark. In their iteration of Chato Santana as El Diablo, Chato loses the *luchador*/cowboy stylizing. He is portrayed as a tattooed East L.A. gangbanger who uses his pyrokinetic powers for criminal gain. However, after he uses his powers to take down a rival gang and realizes he has also scorched and killed innocent women and children, he embarks on a path of redemption.

Figure 20. The final scene of the six-issue series of *El Diablo*, vol. 3, #6 (April 2009).

Figure 21. El Diablo in *New 52 Suicide Squad*, vol. 4, #1 (November 2011).

By the end of the 1980s it seems that DC and Marvel are creating almost exclusively urban-grown-and-inhabiting Latino superheroes. However, with a few exceptions, these urbanized Latinos are one way or another locked into vigilante profiles. The urban Latino superhero performs superheroic deeds to fight urban crime—especially street-level drug dealing—but as outlawed figures trying to bring justice to the people. Latino superheroes either work outside the law or in a world with no laws.

In December 1989, Marvel's creative team Archie Goodwin (writer) and John Byrne (artist) wrap up the decade by adding to the X-Men world the Latina superhero La Bandera (*Wolverine*, vol. 2, #19). They move beyond the individual as vigilante savior of community and characterize her as a revolutionary leader of the people. Daughter of a disillusioned Cuban revolutionary under Fidel Castro, La Bandera grows up in Florida, where her mutant powers activate. She has the power to trigger emotions in people. In the United States she takes on the criminal underworld and its drug dealers (her father ODs on drugs) and leads the common folk to stand in solidarity against exploitation and oppression in the United States and in the fictional Tierra Verde—a South American country ruled by the dictator President Felix Guillermo Caridad; he has connections to the New York criminal underworld. Along the way, she's saved by Wolverine, who helps her fight the supervillain Todd Arliss as Tiger Shark.

Figure 22. La Bandera meets Logan in *Wolverine*, vol. 2, #19 (December 1989).

Unlike Sandoval as El Diablo and other mainstream Latino superheroes who consider the individual act of the vigilante as the way forward to repair a torn social tissue, Goodwin and Byrne's La

Bandera uses her superpowers to help the people organize, resist, and revolt against forces of oppression.

With the exception of La Bandera, the Latinx superheroes who appear in the 1980s as vigilantes pose the problematic question: What is the social validity of vigilantism? Is it socially and morally good or bad? Is it right or wrong to become a vigilante? According not just to local laws or state or federal laws but to the Constitution, it is not just a prerogative but an obligation of the state to protect the citizens of the country, and this protection must be extended to visitors, legal or not.

Bending It à la Latino

As we move into the 1990s, urban-based Latino superheroes become commonplace. And we begin to see a shift in the way comic creators are telling their stories that feature Latinos—and mostly for the better. Likely the result of DC and Marvel attending increasingly to the tremendous innovations taking place in the independent comic scene, with its swiftly growing reader base, this is a period when they began to create more complex Latino superhero comic book storyworlds. Put otherwise, when DC and Marvel transition from making "campy, schlocky stories" to those that take on "real world issues such as addiction, racism and sexuality" (Lawrence, *Storyteller*, 45), we see a greater will to style in the writing and geometrizing of Latino superheroes. In both the writing and the visuals, Latinx superheroes are becoming more complex and engaging in form (the geometric properties) and content (characterization, theme, and plot).

So, while DC and Marvel experienced major setbacks in readership numbers during the 1990s (Marvel even filed for bankruptcy), the radical innovations taking place in the independent comic book publishing scene with publishers like Image (founded in 1992) became a model for fresh comic book creations, including Latino superheroes increasingly created with complex racial, sexual, and class struggles.

In 1990, Marvel's Dann Thomas and Roy Thomas (writers) and Paul Ryan (artist) introduce Miguel Santos as Living Lightning (*Avengers West Coast* #63, October 1990). Much like those Latino superheroes that appeared in the 1980s, Santos is urban: born and raised in East L.A. And while English is the dominant language, he occasionally code-switches with Spanish. He struggles with his Catholic faith. And, like some of his other Latino superhero compadres, he's driven by a hunger to avenge the wrongful death of a family member. His father, Carlos, is killed by the Legion of the Living Lightning gang. Santos comes into his living energy superpower when infiltrating the gang's hideout. This is to say that on first glance there is not much different about Miguel than what's come before in mainstream creations of Latino superheroes. However, as his story unfolds, Marvel introduces an additional layer to his psychology: his closeted gay sexuality. By the time his character arc reaches into the twenty-first century, Dan Slott (writer) and Paul Pelletier (artist) playfully bring him out of the closet. After fighting at the frontlines, then becoming a reservist for Avengers West Coast (Fantastic Four, Doctor Strange, Darkhawk, and Spider-Man), to be able to attend college he travels to visit the GLA and to see if he can join them. When Dr. Ventura as superhero Flatman welcomes Santos, he matter-of-factly states that he thinks the GLA is an acronym for Gay/Lesbian Alliance. Slott chooses to out Living Lightning without much ado. Unlike, say, Extraño, who is *unnaturally* queer, Slott creates Living Lightning as matter-of-fact and naturally queer.

In 1991, Marv Wolfman (writer) and Tom Grindberg (artist) introduce Miriam Delgado as the Latina illusionist Mirage (*New Teen Titans Annual*, vol. 2, #7). Unlike DC's earlier Anglo supervillain Mirage Mike, who uses his powers of illusion to fight Batman (See *Detective Comics* #511, February 1982), Wolfman and Grindberg's Mirage is the leader of the superhero team of new Teen Titans. As her story arc unfolds, we learn that she was a young runaway and kidnap victim in Brazil. And as her character moves into the hands of Phil Jimenez and Jeff Jensen (writers) and Jimenez (artist) in *Team Titans*, "Times Are Far Between (And Few at That)," #13 (October 1993), they choose to hit home hard about what it means to be a Latina in an Anglo, male-dominated superhero universe. In a flashback Jimenez visualizes her being raped by Anglo Deathwing, formerly Dick Grayson as Robin Mirage (*Team Titans*, "You Can't Go Home Again, Part Two," #18, March 1994).

In February 1991, Marv Wolfman (writer) and Tom Grummett (artist) introduce to the New Titans team the Latina Rosabelle Mendez as Pantha (*New Titans*, "Paradise Lost," #73). They create her as a loner, forever estranged from the world (regular people and her fellow Titans), reminding readers of what it means to be Latina in a United States that objectifies and marginalizes women of color. In addition, Wolfman and Grummett flesh out a story that foregrounds heteropatriarchal privilege and violent abuse. Mendez is a human-trafficking victim as well as the subject of physical torture and lab experimentation. It's this experimenting that leads to her transformation into a new ontology: a feline-human hybrid (retractable claws and feet) with great speed, agility, and a heightened sense of sound, smell, and vision. Wolfman literalizes what she already feels herself to be: a Latina sold, owned, and experimented on like an animal. And they turn this scenario around when they make this the source of her superpower. Unfortunately, in 2006 Geoff Johns (writer) and George Pérez (artist) kill her off during the Infinite Crisis; a psychotic Superboy from Earth Prime, who, in yet another expression of Anglo male violence directed at a woman of color, throws a tantrum and rips her head clean off her body (*Infinite Crisis*, vol. 1, "Homecoming," #4, March 2006).

In August 1992, Marvel introduces one of the most interesting Latino superheroes of the early 1990s. *The Amazing Spider-Man* #365 offers a five-page preview of *Spider-Man 2099*, where Peter David (writer) and Rick Leonardi (artist) introduce the mixed Irish and Mexican Miguel "Mig" O'Hara as Spider-Man (Earth-928). (The 2013 published *Spider-Man 2099*, vol. 1, collects issues 1 through 10.) Mig O'Hara takes center stage in the launch of the hugely successful MARVEL 2099 series—a series set in a parallel Earth that extrapolates, then reimagines in a future setting, contemporary political, religious, and economic issues. In the afterword to *Spider-Man 2099* Peter Sanderson writes about how the comic aims to create "a believable future Earth based to a great degree on the political and social trends and scientific developments of the real world in which we live" (236). The introduction of Miguel as Spider-Man could happen because of the way the alternative universes (multiverse) concept opens up possibilities for introducing new characters without having to create them from scratch—something that Marvel, and DC, are rather averse to. We see here the positive potential of the multiverse concept when it comes to creating Latino superheroes. It can, as Kathryn Frank sums up, "provide publishers with a way to experiment with new characters and allow creative teams to change long-standing continuity elements" ("Everybody Wants to Rule the Multiverse: Latino Spider-Men in Marvel's Media Empire," 242).

Under Peter David and Rick Leonardi's skillful verbal and visual storytelling direction, we follow the compelling education of the senses of this Irish-Latino Spidey. At the top of his game intellectually, Miguel runs the genetics division of the megacorporation Alchemax in a dystopic year-2099 set in New York City. This is a Haves (1%) vs. Have-nots (99%) *Blade Runner*–style future, filled with flying vehicles ("Maglevs"), teen cyberpunks, and big brother surveillance systems such as "Public Eye" terrestrial and drone vehicles.

Figure 23. Miguel "Mig" O'Hara as Spider-Man in *Spider-Man 2099* #1 (August 1992).

Miguel's smarts put him in league (albeit tenuous) with the Anglo Haves, who live in the sky-rises high above the racially mixed majority on the streets and in the slums. On one occasion, corporate-paid lackeys known as the Watchdog remark on this part of the city: "Geez, this part of downtown stinks worse everyday" (120). They then corner a single Asian mom, Miss Quan, demanding back rent, while pinning her to the street in an attempt to rape her. And on another end of the twenty-first-century street, mystics proclaim the arrival of the "Age of Heroes," when bygone superheroes like Thor (and not Jesus) will return to save the world: "Thor will be coming, my friends! The time has come for you to repent, for most assuredly . . . The hammer will be falling! And it will crush the unworthy! [. . .] Down with Alchemax! Alchemax must fall!" (229).

However, Miguel's place in the upper echelons of society soon comes to an end. His jealous coworker, Aaron Delgado, sabotages Alchemax's gene alteration machine that causes Miguel's genes to mix with those of a spider. As Kathryn Frank notes, "Although O'Hara has light skin and hair, the visible markers of his spider powers distinguish him from 'normal' society and cause difficulties for him that are easily read as metaphoric of racial/ethnic minority status and the ways in which this difference can be both alienating and empowering. O'Hara not only gains spider powers from his accident but is irreparably physically marked as well" (244). He turns his inhuman features into practical tools and weapons: retracting talons for scaling buildings and webs grown from forearms for abducting bad guys. Once Alchemax's CEO, Tyler Stone, gets wind of the success of the transcoding, he has various supervillains hunt for Miguel O'Hara as Spider-Man. While on the lam, Miguel encounters people and has experiences that begin to open his eyes to the real political and social problems of the world. Along the way, we also learn of his abusive, domineering, mustachioed, macho father, who rules the home like a petty despot. In a flashback, Miguel recalls how he nearly punches the father after telling him: "So I hear you're getting remarried, Dad. Going to make some other woman so crazy that she checks out of reality, you sick . . ." (220). The mom ends up committed to Wellvale Home. And we learn from Miguel's younger brother, Gabriel, that they inherited the father's temper. Gabriel tells Miguel, "Look, I know you're short-tempered. Me too. When you're half Mexican, half Irish, you're not gonna be Mr. Sweetness and Light" (44).

With David's bildungsroman plot and Leonardi's skilled use of panel layout and drawing to geometrize the story, what unfolds is a dynamic and engaging story of Miguel's coming into consciousness of the injustices of the world—something he's largely been sheltered from after having been put into a boarding school (Alchemax funded) for geniuses. Once re-created with the genetic skills of a spider, he becomes an outcast—on the run from Alchemax's hunters—and no longer a member of the 1%. His monstrous ontology—sprouting talons and with spiderlike white pupils—makes Miguel a pariah within his community, too. As an outcast he dons a Spider-Man outfit he picks up for a *Día de los Muertos* celebration in Mexico (42). He reflects, "Wearing it in Mexico for the 'Day of the Dead' festival was one thing, but this . . ." (57). However, that is made of UMF, or unstable molecule fabric, which resists being ripped by his talons and gives him the camouflage needed to hide his identity. As Spider-Man, he directs all of his will and skills to transform this world into a better place. At one point near the end of issue 10, he reflects: "All I ever wanted was to be important. Working for Alchemax was doing the right thing. But I was important to all the wrong people. Being Spider-Man is the wrong thing . . . Law-wise, health-wise . . . But he's important to all the right people. The people I've been working so hard at ignoring. When I put on that costume I start thinking and acting differently. Face it . . . 'Spider-Man' is starting to take over when the mask goes on" (228). As the story unfolds, he becomes aware of how the Spider-Man identity is taking over his civilian persona: "It's looking like Spider-Man doesn't necessarily vanish when the mask comes off. The world we're living in. . . . Gabri saw it. Kasey saw it. Even the crazy lady saw it. If I'm so blasted bright, why didn't I see it until I looked through Spider-Man's eyes?" (228)

This early 1990s epoch marks a significant moment for DC creations. For Ramzi Fawaz, the creation of "The Death of Superman" series in 1992, which led to the re-creating of Superman in a number of different ethnic- and race-identified characters, marks a moment when "minority figures could vie for Superman's vaunted place as an American icon" (*The New Mutants*, 3). Moreover, it marks a moment when creators destabilize and decenter Anglo A-list male superheroes and move more forcefully to its centers those Othered superheroes. The year 1993 is when DC introduces the smartest and most complex of the Latino supervillains: Bane, in *Batman: Knightfall*, vol. 1 (1993–1994). I will go more into his characterization later in the book (especially as it relates to DC's geometrizing of story and the storyfying of geometry in the creating of Bane), but for now, for Chuck Dixon and Doug Moench (writers) as well as Graham Nolan (artist), Bane is the full realization of the antithesis to Bruce Wayne as Batman. That is, Dixon's and Moench's Bane follows the bildungsroman path seen with Miguel O'Hara above (and, of course, Bruce Wayne). However, where those like O'Hara and Wayne follow the path of betterment in terms of the Aristotelian virtue ethics, Bane's is to realize evil. Bane is born on the Hispanophone Caribbean island of Santa Prisca during a moment when state policy is to torture, maim, and destroy psychologically and physically those the state considers its enemies, including Bane's mother. She dies in Peña Duro, where Bane grows up from infancy. He is born with natural cognitive and physical gifts that he grows in the environment of a prison; his self-education includes reading the classics and learning languages (English, Spanish, Portuguese, and Latin), as well as death and murder.

Figure 24. Bane as adult prisoner on Santa Prisca island in *Batman: Knightfall*, vol. 1 (1993).

On one occasion, when he's eight years old, he realizes that to survive this environment he must not only build his strength but also learn to kill. He uses a knife stored inside his *osito* (teddy bear) to kill a bald, predatory thug with an ear-to-nose chain: "We will become friends today, eh? You would like to work for me, would you not, *niño*?" (15). And, as the story unfolds, we experience through the writing and visuals Bane's total education: his senses, mind, and body.

This strength leads the authorities to use him in a dangerous experimental drug procedure; one that kills other prisoners. He survives the drug infusion of "Venom" that gives him super strength, but he's left reliant on the drug. His body needs it every twelve hours or risks death. He uses his smarts and strength to escape Peña Duro and, after he takes revenge on the tyrannical dictator who tortured and killed his father and sentenced his mother and him to life in prison, he makes his way to Gotham to destroy Batman.

Imprinted Latinos

Several of the most creative and complex Latino superheroes of the 1990s appear in two of DC's imprints: Milestone and Wildstorm. Founded in 1993, Milestone comics created one of first extensive, long-running Latino superhero–populated comic books, *Blood Syndicate* (1993–1996). Its Latino superhero team hails from a variety of racial backgrounds (Puerto Rican, Dominican, and African, for instance) and fights equally interesting archenemies, like the Vodun practicing/tech savvy Soul Breaker. Like many of the other superheroes mentioned, they operate outside the law to bring justice to the people; they work to keep the streets clean from the mob, who peddle drugs, as well as from capitalists, who will do anything to move people from their homes to turn profits from urban gentrification. However, creators such as Ivan Velez Jr. (writer) and CrissCross (artist) of *Blood Syndicate* seek to individuate each of the members who make up the Latino superhero team. They are given complex backstories and are invested with psychological and physical challenges (from crack addiction to greed, religious fundamentalism to sexism and internalized racism).

Blood Syndicate also gives full dimension to each team member's struggle with identity, including those informed by gender and sexual orientation as well as desire. For instance, Sara Quiñones as Flashback and her brother Carlos Quiñones as Fade struggle "with the reality of being black and Latino at the same time" (#2, 28). Added to this, Fade struggles with his closeted gay sexuality. The

Puerto Rican superhero Brickhouse struggles with her past as a slave working in the cane fields. And Maria Molina as Aquamaria (with a genetic mutation whereby her body's made of water) struggles with being a social outcast, not just because of her mutation (her mutant-fearing aunt throws her out on the streets) but also because of the ignorance and hostility directed at her for being a monolingual Spanish speaker.

In addition to the Latino characters that populate the Blood Syndicate team, in 1994 Milestone introduces to their universe the dark-skinned, long-haired Latino Miguel as the eponymous masked vigilante Kobalt. In this sixteen-issue run, eponymously titled comic, *Kobalt*, John Rozum (writer) and Arvell Jones (artist) model Kobalt after other self-taught Latino superheroes mentioned earlier, like El Diablo. However, Kobalt is a much more sinister, darker vigilante, styled more after the likes of Bane in terms of musculature and rage, but with a progressive mission: to use his self-taught, pole-wielding fight skills to take down street thugs and multinational corporate evildoers, such as Milton St. Cloud and other criminals who inhabit Dakota City. However, where the others either die or simply fizzle out and disappear, Milestone creators not only bring this bildungsroman to a full close but do so by imbuing Kobalt with a fresh awareness of his role as a lone-acting vigilante. After a near-death battle with a supervillain, he learns that he alone cannot save the world; that this will take the work of the masses.

Wildstorm introduced several significant Latino superheroes in the mid- to late 1990s. In 1995, Brandon Choi (writer) and J. Scott Campbell (artist) create Hector Morales as Powerhouse—a code-switching Latino superhero of mixed German/Argentinian ancestry with the most unusual superpower: he can track people by reading traces left by their emotions and, as well, use the emotions of others (and his own) to charge up and increase muscle mass (*Gen*[13], vol. 2, #7, 1995). One way or another, Choi and Campbell identify the emotion system as his source of power. Moreover, like Kobalt and O'Hara as Spider-Man, Powerhouse is conflicted over his role as a mercenary or vigilante. Before being killed during a mission against the villain Gnome, he turns to alcohol to drown out the memory of terrible deeds done for the mercenary team known as DV8.

In May 1999, Warren Ellis (writer) and Bryan Hitch (artist) introduce to the DC universe one of the most complex and interesting Latina superheroes: Dr. Angela "Angie" Spica. She's one of the founding members of superhero team The Authority (*Authority* #1). They anchor her firmly in an urban environment and with working-class roots. She is one of six children, whose father works as a bus driver and her mother at a launderette to make ends meet. While Ellis and Hitch slip a little into cliché when they invest her with a stereotypical hothead temperament, especially as associated with desire (she tries to kill her lover, Captain Atom, when she spots him with another woman), their forceful identification of Angie as a Latina deeply committed to her family and her own education tilt the balance back. She remains one of mainstream comics' smartest and most dynamic superheroes. Indeed, not only do her genius-level smarts and hard work land her a doctorate in engineering, but she develops a liquid nanotechnology that gives her the power to turn her body into liquid metal and to create weaponry, additional copies of herself—and whatever the nanotechnology and her imagination will allow.

Back to DC and Marvel Business

Not all of the comics created in the 1990s with a Latino-bent enriched the palette of Latino representation. Indeed, while DC and Marvel certainly created their share of Latino superheroes as light-skinned (or *güero*), it is not until 1996 that we see the first Anglo superhero dressed in, say, brown face. For DC, Grant Morrison (writer) and Mark Millar (artist) invent the blond-locked medical physician Curt Falconer as Aztek (*Aztek, The Ultimate Man* #1, August 1996). Physically trained in the art of combat south of the U.S.-Mexico border by the secret Q Society, he returns to the U.S. city of Vanity ready to fight crime while sporting a costume modeled after the Aztec warrior god Quetzalcoatl. His winged suit of armor and sunray-shaped helmet enhance his cognitive, sensory, and physical abilities. The Anglo Falconer in his Aztek gear becomes the über-savior: at one point he saves not only Vanity but also the entire planet.

Figure 25. Aztek in *Aztek, The Ultimate Man* #1 (August 1996).

In 1996, several new Latinos were born—and reborn. DC's Chuck Dixon (writer) and Robert Campanella (artist) give the Green Lantern a Latino makeover with Kyle Rayner's backstory, which includes his estranged Mexican father, Gabriel Vasquez; because of his work for the Mexican CIA and to save his family from imminent danger, he changes his name to Aaron Rayner and leaves three-year-old Kyle and his mother, Maria (*Green Arrow* #111, August 1996).

Figure 26. Green Lantern's Mexican papa, Gabriel Vasquez, in *Green Arrow* #111 (August 1996).

And Karl Kesel (writer) and Steve Mattsson (artist) give a Latino makeover to erstwhile Anglo superhero Hero when they re-create him as urban-born Afrolatino Hero Cruz (*Superboy and the Ravers* #1, September 1996). After Superboy follows Canadian superhero Sparx to a rave filled with all sorts that don't speak English, Hero arrives on the scene.

Like Vibe and other Latino superheroes that came before, Hero's associated with music; in this case, a rave that's identified by Kindred Marx as an "Event Horizon" (13). His outfit and slang locate him racially and as urban: he sports hybrid football gear and baggy overalls with hip-hop-style sneakers, as well as a six-o'-clock shadow and a gold earring—not the usual leotard getup of the superhero. And Superboy's surprised to hear that Hero speaks English: "Hold it . . . you speak English! That's almost stranger than everything else here!" (11). Hero responds in nonstandard English: "Oh, you ain't seen nothin' yet!" (11).

Figure 27. Hero's first appearance in *Superboy and the Ravers* #1 (September 1996).

As this story unfolds, readers learn that the Latino Hero Cruz is a petty thief. He comes across the Hero Dial ("H-Dial") artifact by more illicit means than the Anglo teen Robby Reed, who discovers it in a cavern. And, unlike the earlier Anglo iteration of Hero, Hero Cruz becomes entangled in all sorts of sexuality and gender issues that the Latino Cruz does when he dials H-E-R-O on the Hero Dial. He, too, comes into superpowers, but in ways that trouble rigid identifications of sexuality. That is, his power allows him to assume the persona (to transform for an hour into a new superhero with new superpowers, but never twice) of others who are heterosexual, even though he's gay, leading to all sorts of configurations of straight and gay expressions of desire. So when Canadian superhero Sparx thinks he's interested in her romantically, he's only interested because he has taken on the traits of a straight superhero.

This same year DC added another disabled Latino superhero to their superhero roster. In the nine-issue run of *Firebrand* (#1, February 1996) Brian Augustyn (writer) and Sal Velluto (artist, who also worked on *Moon Knight*) bring the former Anglo (Golden Age: 1938–1945) superhero Firebrand back into play as the Cuban New York detective, ponytailed and brown-skinned Alejandro "Ally" Sanchez.

Figure 28. Alejandro "Ally" Sanchez as Firebrand in *Firebrand* #2 (February 1996).

He's filled with guilt over the loss of his sister, Christina, burned alive in a fire. "Unlike Christina, of course, I survived this horrible night" (6). As *Firebrand* unfolds, we learn of his estrangement from his *familia*, including his brother, Javier, a priest, and of his obsession with finding kidnapped children. His fridge is chock-full of milk cartons with photos and "Have You Seen Me?" His booby-trapped answering machine leads to an explosion in his apartment and him losing his legs. While in a coma he has a vision of his sister, who tells him, "Now is not your time and you must go back to your good work . . . te amo hermano, mío" (6–7). Local

Anglo philanthropist Noah Hightower funds a superpowered suit that not only allows Sanchez to walk again but also gives him super strength and speed and emits a green flame.

Much like Marv Wolfman (writer) and Jerry Ordway's (artist) backstory to Gangbuster (1987), Sanchez's cybernetic prosthetic legs and cybernetic-enhanced armor get him back on the streets, not as a detective but as Firebrand. However, he soon discovers that the corporate benefactor who paid for his bionic reengineering is Noah Hightower, who lost his own son twenty-five years before—and his wife from grief. "Since then, I've devoted myself to finding ways to ensure that no more children—no more victims—suffer" (15). When he introduces Alejandro to a way to modify further his bionic equipment with a technologically advanced suit, he tells him, "I want this agent to be a force of good . . . In short, I'm looking for a hero" (14).

Augustyn and Velluto create a Cuban American Latino super-hero whose family (memory of his sister) and his priest brother, Javi, function as a kind of moral compass, reminding him of right (jus-tice) and wrong (vengeance) and not to get swept into vengeance for vengeance's sake. In an interesting twist that complicates Javi's characterization, he himself takes the life of a bad guy: "Your power comes from being plugged straight into hell—and that connection has to be severed now. God forgive us all" ("Saints and Sinners," #6, July 1996, 21). For the rest of the issues Javi struggles with having taken a person's life, until his sister, Christina, appears to him in a vision: "If you need forgiveness, Javi, all you have to do is accept it. . . . Open your heart, Javi. . . . Let the light in" ("Final Notice," #9, October 1996, 8). Moreover, he emerges from his rebirth at once vulnerable (he walks with a cane) and, when he's suited up, embodying positively the stereotype of the fiery Latino. After his first energy, supercharged boost "relayed and downloaded via a Hightower orbital satellite" (20), he remarks, "Nobody warned me about the fire . . . My god, the fire." (19). He continues, "There's no way to describe the exhilaration . . . It was as if the fire was set loose in my blood. . . . I felt incredible, unstoppable!" (21).

Alejandro as Firebrand is a cross between vigilante superhe-roes like Ghost Rider (fire), Spawn (mask), and Cyborg (body). When his brother, Javi, asks him if he's after vengeance, he says, "No, Javi, justice . . . Believe me, Javi, I'm no monster. . . . I'm on the side of the angels" ("Burning Bright," #2, March 1996, 9–10). As such, he doesn't so much replicate the stereotype of Latinos as *hot* and fiery, but embodies this stereotype in ways that lead to setting straight racial injustices. He uses his powers to protect the innocent and vulnerable (he finds the multiethnic band of "snatched kids" in "The Best of Families" [#3, April 1996]) from a team of genetically enhanced, blond, Aryan, young supervillains, such as Sarah, Kyra, Aaron, Simon, and Sebastian. Augustyn and Velluto repeatedly link the supervillains to the eugenics of Nazism.

The theme of whites against people of color arises again in *Firebrand*, "Children of the Damned," #7 (August 1996). The issue opens with a panel that shows two African Americans parked next to a sign that features two white children and that reads: "Welcome to Beacon Hill: Home of the Best Kids in America." A group of well-dressed white teens arrive on the scene and beat up the two men of color. Once they've stuffed the bodies of the two men in the trunk, one of the white teens tells another, "Tommy, you drive these fellows a ways down the road . . . Far enough to keep Beacon Hill out of their obituaries."

And, Augustyn and Velluto build into Firebrand's characterization a struggle with his Latinoness both in the form of his connection to Catholicism (his struggle with his brother, Javi, who is a priest in "Guardian Angels," #4) and his own machismo. After a conversation with his father, who asks him why he's still "chasing the bad guys" after being blown up by those "sinvergüenzas," Alejandro reflects to himself, "I'm still not sure why I didn't mention the pain that still knifed through every inch of my body. Macho, maybe. . . . Or fear that they'd take this gift away from me" ("Killer's Garden," #5). In spite of providing a complex Latino superhero that generated a lot of interest and a growing readership, DC canned *Firebrand*. The series ended with Alejandro's interior monologue: "And so that adventure ended . . . in peace. There were many, many more—but those are tales for another time . . . Adios" ("Final Notice," #9, August 1996). In the reader comments at the end of the final issue, Brian Augustyn writes, "We can blame it on the market, we can blame it on low sales, we can blame it on the weather, but we can't say we didn't do our darnedest" (*Firebrand* #9, August 1996).

Figure 29. Firebrand vs. Anglo racist robotic teens in *Firebrand* #7 (August 1996).

Toward the end of the 1990s, Marvel introduces not only a highly educated Afrolatina, Dr. Cecilia Reyes, to the X-Men story-world (*X-Men*, vol. 2, #65, June 1997), but also one of the most fascinating and compelling Latina superheroes to date, Joe Quesada's mestiza, Maya Lopez as Echo (*Daredevil*, vol. 2, #9, December 1999). Both Latina superheroes suffer from the loss of their fathers: at age six Reyes sees her father gunned down in a drive-by shooting where she lives in the Bronx; Lopez loses her father to the murderous kingpin Fisk, who, after he adopts her, blames the father's murder on Daredevil. Both Latinas choose to hang up the garbs of civilian life—Lopez was an extraordinary concert pianist and Reyes was a trauma surgeon. Both use their smarts and strengths to subdue bad guys. Reyes uses her mutant powers, which allow her to project a force field around her body, and Echo her uncanny knack at mimicry, a photographic reflex that, when she studies VHS tapes of martial arts fights (including those of *Daredevil*), allows her to become an expert martial artist. While both are compelling, strong, and smart Latina superheroes, Joe Quesada (artist) and David Mack's (writer/artist) Echo takes it to the next level. These creators complicate notions of what it means to be Latina, identifying Maya Lopez's roots (at least on her father's side) in an indigenous ancestry. They also do something very creative with their introduction of her as a disabled Latina superhero—she's not differently abled physically in the way that we've seen with Gangbuster or Firebrand, for instance. She's born deaf. It is her deafness that propels her education of all her other senses in this bildungsroman.

Figure 30. Maya Lopez's education of the senses in *Daredevil, Vol. 2: Parts of a Hole* (2003).

Not only does she learn to "hear" the piano through sight and touch, but she also becomes a highly skilled acrobat and a gifted ballerina. This allows her to begin to embody a physical body that feels like an echo—as if she's not quite *in* her body. This is especially reflected in the art of both collections, *Daredevil, Vol. 2: Parts of a Hole* (2003) and *Daredevil: Vision Quest* (2015), in which her story doesn't follow the six-panel layout (rather we see action flowing across panels) and where often a background visual depicts other layers to her psychology, like picture frames, childhood sketches, collages, Picasso-like art samples, a collection of mouths, or other symbols. Indeed, as David Mack (writer) remarks in the introduction to *Daredevil: Parts of a Hole*: "It wasn't until I saw Joe's first penciled pages of my script that I truly felt that the story succeeded at meeting those challenges. Joe's artwork brought the story to life, and made it breathe in a way . . . His art in this story knows when to whisper, and it knows when to scream."

Figure 31. Maya Lopez's superhero bildungsroman in *Daredevil, Vol. 2: Parts of a Hole* (2003).

We see the presence of will to style in form and content throughout Quesada and Mack's creation of Maya Lopez as the superhero Echo. It's as if her character is so compelling that it drives other creators to step up to the high bar set by Quesada and Mack. For instance, in Brian Michael Bendis (writer) and Alex Maleev's (artist) *The New Avengers Revolution* we meet her once again, this time in Japan as the yakuza warrior known as Ronin. In the opening pages, she reflects, "No one looks at the girls. They're just objects. I could sit there, like a piece of giggling furniture . . .

Not as Echo, not as Maya Lopez, but as someone they don't know, someone they couldn't trace back. As a man. As a figure of shadows. As you." This is integrated with visuals that not only move the story forward but also enrich and give further dimension to what Echo says herself. Indeed, with the character Echo, Marvel creates a mestiza superhero who is finally given a complex and compelling characterization and story line.

Before closing the book on the 1990s, I will mention briefly Kurt Busiek (writer) and Brent Anderson's (artist) *Astro City* #13, published in 1998. Busiek and Anderson create Latino superhero Esteban Rodrigo Suarez Hidalgo as El Hombre, but in a time and setting of the Silver Age of comics (1956–1969). That is, they create a retrospective comic book storyworld that retrofits this period of comics with more Latino superheroes. Cut from the same cloth as The Whip and El Gaucho, Esteban Rodrigo Suarez Hidalgo is not hurting for money. However, while he is heir to a silver mine, he chooses not to follow in his father's footsteps. Rather, he chooses to look to his circus performer uncle as a role model. He becomes an adept acrobatic athlete and wielder of whips. As the muscled, Zorro-style, masked, black-and-red-spandexed El Hombre, he uses his fighting skills and titanium whip to clean up "The Barrio" of Astro City. He eventually becomes disenchanted with his role as a vigilante in a world that refuses to change for the better, and withdraws from society as a recluse.

Twenty-First-Century Multiplicities

As one might expect in terms of sociohistorical circumstances, it is not until the last decade of the twentieth century that we begin to see the kind of rich and complex Latinx superhero of an Echo or an O'Hara, for instance. This widening of a spectrum of vibrant bandwidths in the creation of Latino superheroes continues in the first decade of the twenty-first century.

This coincides historically with the massive growth in the demographic presence of Latinos in the United States. With our number rising daily, not only have we become the majority in places like California and the Southwest generally, but with our demographic growth (and this is happening fastest in the Midwest and the South) we are the majority minority in the United States generally. To put it otherwise, when superheroes like Firebird and Vibe appeared in the 1980s, there were approximately 14.6 million Latinos in the United States. With the creation of today's Latino superheroes, Latinos number in the 51 million, not including our 12 million undocumented brothers and sisters. And with this browning of the United States we also see a greater number of Latinos (especially artists) *creating* content for DC and Marvel. That is, we see a greater will to style in the making of superhero comics that distills and reconstructs the identities and experiences of Latinos in engaging and complex ways.

In 2000, the DC team Oscar Pinto (writer) and Giovanni Barberi and F. G. Haghenbeck (artists) introduce bilingual Latina Andrea Rojas as Ácrata in *Superman Annual*, vol. 2, #12 (August 2000). She appears in the foreground of the Mexican flag (red, white, and green and with the eagle/snake symbol) and spread over a map of Mexico. Along with Imán and El Muerto, she's featured as one of "The Newest Heroes South of the Border!" And once inside the storyworld proper, the creators willfully put Mexico at its center. We're not in an Anglo-dominant U.S. metropolis; we're in Mexico, where Clark Kent's covering a story for *El Planeta*. Oscar Pinto writes Superman as a Spanish speaker (the < > brackets indicate this), and gives Lois the capacity for Spanglish ("Hasta luego, sweetie"). In addition to the recentering of plot and character, where Mexico and Mexicans are no longer just backdrop material, the artist team gives Superman *and* Lois Lane a brown phenotypic makeover. Moreover, the story features a team of Mexican-based superheroes. After Superman's taken out by a young girl with telekinetic, magical abilities, Ácrata, Imán, and El Muerto come to Superman's rescue.

Oscar Pinto, however, doesn't write them as the brown servants (or janitors) to Anglo A-lister Superman as one might expect, given the long tradition of this that dates back to even before Marvel's Firebird in the 1980s. They are the center of the story, and remain so till the story's conclusion. Additionally, Pinto invests them not only with smarts (Imán is a former astronaut and a Yale Ph.D., and Ácrata is super literate and knows well her ancient and contemporary Mexican history . . . she even names her cat Zapata), but also with a critical sensibility that calls attention to

Figure 32. Acrata, Imán, and El Muerto rescue Superman in
Superman Annual, vol. 2, #12 (August 2000).

how Superman has been traditionally used as an appendage to U.S.
imperialism. (Notably, in some re-creations of Superman we see
him grow weary with being cast in this do-gooder-cum-imperialist
role. For instance, in *Action Comics* #900, he renounces his U.S.
citizenship at the UN.)

In addition to Ácrata's propensity to willy-nilly quote lines of
poetry (even graffitiing them on random walls), she sleuths out
bad guys by deciphering Mexican symbols like Ometeotl as the
"God of the near and close"; she's also independent and self-suffi-
cient, using more of her self-trained warrior martial arts skills than

superpowers generated from Mayan supernaturalism. Pinto makes Ácrata and the other south-of-the-border superheroes Spanish speakers (the use of the < > is an indication of this). Barberi and Haghenbeck's costumes visualize these Latino superheroes as rooted in distant (pre-Colombian mythological) and proximate (*luchador*) ancestry: Ácrata's full-body spandex suit features Mayan symbols, El Muerto sports a homemade *luchador* outfit, and Imán's self-designed-and-created high-tech armored suit includes its own set of pre-Colombian symbols. In the end, Ácrata and her team save Superman, Mexico, and the entire planet from total destruction.

Figure 33. Acrata swings atop Mexico's skyline in *Superman Annual*, vol. 2, #12 (August 2000).

Not all creations during this period were as willfully done. In September 2000, DC introduced the south-of-the-border Latinx superhero team known as Super Malon in *Flash Annual*, vol. 2, #13. Unlike Ácrata, El Muerto, and Imám, Chuck Dixon (writer) and Enrique Alcatena (artist) create a lackluster set of hybrid and bruja superheroes: El Lobizon, El Bagual, Cachiru, La Salamanca, El Pampero, Vizacacha, and Cimarron. This creative team (clichéd writing and static, flat visuals) takes Latino superheroes back decades.

In March 2001, Joe Kelly (writer), along with Doug Mahnke and Lee Bermejo (artists), introduces Pamela as Menagerie in

Figure 34. El Lobizon, El Bagual, Cachiru,
La Salamanca, El Pampero, Vizacacha,
and Cimarron in *Flash Annual*, vol. 2, #13
(September 2000).

Action Comics #775, "What's So Funny About Truth, Justice &
the American Way?" Kelly writes her as of Puerto Rican origin
and, postinfection by alien symbeasts, she becomes a member of
Manchester Black's metahuman "Elite" team. (In 2004, we meet
Pamela's twin, Sonja, in *Justice League of America* #100.) Mahnke
and Bermejo visualize her as a light shade of brown skin with curly
hair, but with Caucasian facial features, busty, and exotic: her
body's epidermal layer crawls with symbiotic, parasitic symbeasts.
She's sexualized and exoticized (*alienized*), and threatens to *infect*
those around her with the poison of the symbeasts. However, like
some of the smart creations of Latina superheroes that predate
Pamela, she at once embodies the pervading stereotypes (sexual
and animalistic) *and* uses them. She can detach from her body
the parasitic symbeasts and use them to fight her Anglo enemies,
including A-listers like Superman.

This same year, Geoff Johns (writer) and Latino Ralph "Rags" Morales (artist) introduce to the DC universe the supervillain-cum-superhero Alexander "Alex" Montez (*JSA*, vol. 2, #26–27, 2001).

Figure 35. Pam as Menagerie in *Action Comics*, vol. 1, #775 (March 2001).

Enraged at the murder of his cousin, Yolanda (a Latina discussed earlier in this chapter), and teaming up with his love interest, the genetically engineered assassin Sosesh Mykros, known as Nemesis, Montez fights world criminal organizations with the ultimate goal of avenging her death. And while at first Johns creates him as a stereotypical hotheaded Latino—he "reacts with emotion, not logic"—he learns to use his reason system to control Eclipso's destructive spirit and power; after stealing the black diamond that holds Eclipso's soul, he at first is controlled by Eclipso through the "binding glyphs" tattooed all over Montez's body (he kills Nemesis), but in the end he uses his brain's reason system to make the hard and terminal decision: to end his own life in order to destroy Eclipso. He takes his own life in order to stop Eclipso from wreaking havoc on humanity as a whole.

Figure 36. Alex Montez jumps to his death after murdering his love interest, Nemesis, in *JSA, Vol. 8: Black Reign* (July 2005).

As his suicide scene demonstrates, the artist team's careful use of geometric shapes (buildings, his body, and the concentric shapes he leaves upon impact), angle (long, medium, and close shots), layout (rhythm and size of panels), the brown, blue, purple, and magenta colors, and the thick black-inked gutters all add up to a powerful storytelling moment that drives home the tragedy of his life. This is made all the more tragic when we see Eclipso's spirit still alive in the black diamond (where he'd been trapped before) that falls from Montez's lifeless hand. The visuals combine with a plot and characterization that move the story forward with great intensity.

Certainly Montez is formed by experiences that are much richer than those of his Latino superhero predecessors. And we see, too, how form and content interact in inseparable ways to convey this more complex Latino character who teeter-totters between good and bad in his codes of behavior. We see the willful integration of geometry into the creating of Montez, who has to literally manipulate the geometric shapes on his body to control his superpowers; he's also a superhero not so unlike Ghost Rider, whose complexity grows from his deep conflicts between doing good and doing evil in the world. Montez commits suicide in order *not* to bring more harm to the world.

Figure 37. Renée Montoya is outed as a lesbian in *Gotham Central*, vol. 1, #6 (June 2003).

While not a superhero per se, in 2003, Latina (Dominican) DC's Renée Montoya does use her wits, sharpshooter skill (an advanced energy pistol), and acrobatic strength to fight crime in *Gotham Central*, vol. 1 (2003). Here Greg Rucka and Ed Brubaker (writers) as well as Michael Lark (artist) move a Latina from comic book margins (*Batman*, vol. 1, #475, March 1992) to the center. Rucka and Brubaker innovatively write her as a Latina lesbian outed at her police headquarters by a photo of her kissing another woman (*Gotham Central*, vol. 1, #6, June 2003). She is disavowed and disowned by her Catholic family. She resigns from the police force.

In issue 7 of Geoff Johns, Greg Rucka, Grant Morrison, and Mark Waid's fifty-two-issue comic book series, *52* (May 2006–May 2007), Katherine "Kate" Kane (Batwoman) and Renée Montoya kiss.

Figure 38. Katherine "Kate" Kane (Batwoman) and Renée Montoya kiss in *52*, vol. 1, #7 (June 2006).

That DC creates a Latina lesbian superhero is remarkable. However, as Jonathan Risner observes, the story line subordinates her Latinaness. We know she's Latina mostly because of her name. Indeed, as Risner speculates, perhaps the creating of a character who is fleshed out equally as Latina and lesbian is too much for DC. Cynically, he wonders if perhaps DC is only willing to go for "one niche market at a time" ("'Authentic' Latinas/os and Queer Characters in Alternative and Mainstream Comics," 47).

However, Renée Montoya comes into her own as a Latina and lesbian superhero in *The Question: Pipeline* (2011). Greg Rucka (writer) and Cully Hamner (artist) write and geometrize her as tough (posture), dark brown (phenotype), without spandex (instead, fedora, suit or leather jacket with jeans or baggy khakis), and bilingual (English and Spanish). They embrace her lesbian and Latina identity. She fights crime in the barrio where she speaks mostly Spanish (indicted by the <> used around her English phrases). And, they create a story line where she takes down Vargas and his crew; he runs a sex-trafficking operation that exploits young Latinas crossing the border from crime-ridden countries south of the U.S.-Mexico border.

Certainly Marvel seems to have a better track record of creating superheroes that are equaled by their gender, sexuality, and

Figure 39. Renée Montoya as The Question discovers a sex-trafficking operation in *The Question: Pipeline* (2011).

Figure 40. Renée Montoya as The Question gets ready to fight gangbangers in *The Question: Pipeline* (2011).

Figure 41. Renée Montoya liberates young Latinas in *The Question: Pipeline* (2011).

ethnicity. Think Maya Lopez as Echo or Miguel O'Hara as Spider-Man. However, Marvel creators have also produced some doozies. In 2003, Peter Miligan (writer) and Mike Allred (artist) introduce the urban-dwelling Latino skateboarder Robert "Robbie" Rodriguez as El Guapo to the X-Static team (*X-Static* #9, April 2003). While Allred pays attention to details like his skater look (slip-on Vans, jeans, and bandana), he subordinates Robbie's Latinoness. His Caucasian features and light brown skin dominate any other markers of ethnicity: dark hair, brown eyes, and shadow goatee. Miligan does write him as bilingual. On one occasion, he remarks, "You'd think being fluent in English and Spanish would be enough, but no. I gotta learn Doop-Speak."

He feels marginalized less as a Latino and more as a mutant. When he decides to join the X-Static mutant team he tells

Figure 42. Robbie Rodriguez as "El Guapo" and a lothario in *X-Static* #9 (April 2003).

Consuela, his Latina girlfriend: "I'm a mutant. I'm different. I've been called that all my life. And this is the only way I can use it." Indeed, Milligan decides to identify Robbie's Latinoness as his humanness, but a stereotypical Latinoness: his macho, hypersexual drive. When he can't resist women, he self-identifies as human. On one such occasion, he ponders, "Three in a bed last night. That's right. Same as usual." And on another (figure 43) he lets himself off the hook for sleeping around, and behind the back of his

Figure 43. Robbie Rodriguez is beaten up by his skateboard for cheating on Consuela in *X-Static* #9 (April 2003).

anthropomorphic skateboard and his Latina girlfriend, Consuela, by telling himself: "I'm only human . . ."

In 2003, Marvel introduced a far more interesting Latino superhero: U.S.-born, South American–raised Latino Manuel Diego Armand Vincent as Junta (*The Crew*, July 2003–January 2004). Christopher Priest writes him as a smart former military officer (Los Cuarenta Ladrones and U.S. intelligence agent) who ends up in Queens, looking for work as a mercenary. And Joe Bennett visualizes him as a brown-skinned, steadfastly planted on the earth, full-bodied Latino who sports baggy fatigues. Both Priest and Bennett give an innovative new spin on the Latino as-only-body stereotype. His superpower: a body that bends space and time to the point of total implosion of all that exists within an eight-mile radius.

In the same year (and month) that Junta appears, Brian K. Vaughan (writer) and Adrian Alphona (artist) introduce another Latino teen, Victor Mancha, in their *Runaways* series. With Mancha's origin story Vaughn takes us into new territory; we learn that his mother, Marianella Mancha, is a victim of cartel crime and exploitation; she is forced to use her body to smuggle drugs into the United States. Legally and biologically unable to adopt, Ultron fuses her DNA with cybernetic parts to create Victor. That is, Vaughn writes and Alphona visualizes a character who embodies the in-between-ness of Latino existence. It's this essential in-between-ness or hybridity that becomes Victor's power.

In 2005, Marvel grows yet another innovative hybrid teen superhero, the mixed Puerto Rican and Mexican Anya Corazon as Araña. In the manga-pocket-book series (*The Heart of the Spider*, *Night of the Hunter*, and *Civil War*) Fiona Avery (writer) and Mark Brooks (artist) anchor her firmly in her Latino identity: she's deeply connected to her cultural roots via the memory of her Mexican mother, Sofia, and she learns much from her smart, sensitive, and strong Puerto Rican father, an investigative reporter for the *New York Herald*. In "Anya (Sofía Araña) Corazón," Isabel Millán discusses how the creators of the character use her marginality as a Latina (Puerto Rican and Mexican) to destabilize fixed notions of what it means to be Latina. Millán also details the parental tensions present in Anya's characterization as a Latina: the spirit of her deceased mother encourages her to embrace her spider-power matrilineage versus an overprotective father who wants to keep her close to home. And, Avery and Brooke allow Anya to breathe as the central protagonist of her own generously expansive story. Avery writes her as smart and culturally and racially aware. Brooke visualizes her as strong, agile, and with a non-spandexed costume: urban baggy street wear that comfortably allows for her spider-exoskeleton armor to wrap her body. And, while Avery and Brooke invest her with spiderlike superpowers, through discipline and training she becomes a fierce warrior who knows well how to battle with punches and kicks enemies like the Sisterhood of the Wasp.

Figure 44. Anya Corazon transforming into Araña in
Araña: The Heart of the Spider, vol. 1 (March 2005).

While a marginal character within the Marvel universe, Anya is one of the few Latina superhero characters who evolve. While most of those I've discussed in mainstream comics remain the same age throughout their story arcs, Marvel follows Anya as she grows from tween to late teen. In *Spider-Girl: Family Values* (2011) Paul Tobin (writer), along with Clayton Henry and Pepe Larraz (artists), fully fleshes Anya out as the Latina superhero Spider-Girl. With Tobin and the art team making her the protagonist of her own story (and series), we see the development of a superhero anchored in an urban, contemporary Latinidad. She's dark-skinned and visually shown battling evil in and around a vibrant urban environment. And she's contemporary: she tweets @The_Spider_Girl. (Marvel keeps a live Tumblr page that expands the Spider-Girl universe: http://spidette.tumblr.com/.)

Figure 45. Anya tweets @The_Spider_Girl in *Spider-Girl: Family Values,* #1 (January 2011).

In 2005, second-generation Cuban American Joe Quesada introduces to the Daredevil world the Yoruban-superpowered team known as the Santerians: disillusioned civil rights activist Nestor Rodriguez/NeRo as Eleggua, who can scramble thoughts and communication; the Afrolatino Ogun, with superhuman strength; Changó, who shoots fire to manipulate all forms of liquid; and the Afrolatino Oya, who can control the weather (*Daredevil,* "Father," #2, October 2005). Adilifu Nama and Maya Hadad identify the Santerians as Marvel's "staunch foray into the borderlands of

Afrolatino representation of superheroes" ("Mapping the *Blatino* Badlands and Borderlands of American Pop Culture," 258). They further remark on how Ogun articulates most clearly the intersection of blackness and Latinoness while the other superheroes "shade" more ethnically toward the Latino end of the ethnoracial phenotypic spectrum (259). As I discuss in *Your Brain on Latino Comics*, the characters are shaped by the syncretic cultural and religious practices of the Afrolatino Caribbean; Joe Quesada's inclusion of a glossary of Santeria terms at the end of the volume that includes issues 1 through 6, *Daredevil: Father* (2009), invites readers to understand the historical weight and significance of these superheroes powers within a colonial and postcolonial context. They go

Figure 46. Santerians: Afrolatino superheroes in *Daredevil*, "Father," #2 (October 2005).

mano a mano with Irish American Daredevil, who has been pushing crime from Hell's Kitchen to the Latino barrio that they've been trying to defend and heal. In "The Alien Is Here to Stay," Mauricio Espinoza identifies the tension between Daredevil and the Afrolatino Santerians as revealing the problems of segregation within cities (comic book and otherwise) and also the inadequacy of Anglo superheroes to stop crime and their refusal to "protect an increasingly diverse city" (197).

Through coloring and visuals (Ogun's cornrows, for instance) Quesada seeks to re-create the complex ways Latinos look and exist in the world, to show how, for some Latinos, there's a long and deep history of cultural and biological mixing between our African, indigenous, and Spanish ancestry. Moreover, he creates a panoply of Latino superheroes who derive their power from this biological and cultural syncretism.

In May 2004, DC team Will Pfeifer (writer) and Patrick Gleason (artist) introduce the *morena* (or dark-skinned) Lorena Marquez as Aquagirl on New Earth (*Aquaman*, vol. 6, #16). Pfeifer creates her as an orphan: after a huge earthquake (triggered by scientist Anton Geist) sinks San Diego into the ocean, Marquez is the only one of her family saved—by Aquaman. Indeed, after he nurses her back to health, Marquez discovers she can breathe under water. She and Aquaman rebuild the city as Sub Diego. To fight crime in this new city, Marquez dons an aquatic costume and assumes the identity of Aquagirl.

Figure 47. Aquagirl in *Aquaman*, vol. 6, #32 (September 2005).

In writing (Pfeifer) and geometric shaping (Gleason) there's less interest in emphasizing her battle strength and skill and more interest in her as a sex object. Pfeifer writes her as hypersexual, jumping on any and all males she can get her hands on, including

Blue Beetle and an already hitched Superboy; this latter of her trysts leads to her expulsion from the Teen Titan team.

Figure 48. Birth of Antoñio Stark in *Ultimate Iron Man*, vol. 1 (2006).

In October 2006, Orson Scott Card created in Marvel's Ultimate line of comics the Latino Iron Man as Antoñio Stark. To throw the net wide to attract new generations of young readers to comics (the original Marvel universe had become so cluttered with story lines), in 2001 Marvel executive Bill Jemas's launch of the Marvel Ultimate universe opened up the possibility for these kinds of ethnically marked avatars of A-list originals, something that we see play out to positive effect later with the introduction of the Blatino Miles Morales as Spider-Man. As Derek Johnson sums up, Marvel Ultimate titles turned back clocks to origins "to tell their old stories in a new way" (73). In Card's Ultimate storyworld he creates a Howard Stark having married again, this time to a light-skinned Latina biogenetics genius, Dr. Maria Cerrera. Card's origin story: after Cerrera's genetic modification she dies while giving birth to a baby boy. On her deathbed she explains to Howard how "undifferentiated neural tissue will grow all through his body. As if this whole body is brain. Greater mental capacity. Quicker. Like no human in history" (19). Howard names him Antoñio, after Maria's deceased brother. However, because Antoñio was born with his entire epidermal layer as his brain, Howard has to invent a liquid, biological armor (made out of genetically modified bacteria that group together and dissipate kinetic energy upon impact) to ease the agony experienced when he's touched.

Orson Scott Card exercises his counterfactual capacity here to radically overturn a long tradition of stereotypes: the Latino as only body and no brain. Rather than the Latino superhero appearing as *all* ruled by the corporeal (uncontrolled desire or out of control physical violence), Card invents Antoñio Stark as a body that is *all brain*. Card has Antoñio grow up to become a teen, then goateed Latino, who uses his super-epidermal brain power to outwit racist criminals and bring to justice racially motivated criminals. Notably, Marvel's interest in turning tables with the Iron Man narrative continues today with the introduction of fifteen-year-old African American Riri Williams. Brian Michael Bendis writes her as a genius prodigy attending MIT who figures out how to reverse engineer the Iron Man suit. And while artist Stefano Caselli portrays her as African American (and not a character with Anglo bone features in blackface) and has her proudly rooted in her African

Figure 49. Antoñio Stark as Iron Man in *Ultimate Comics Iron Man* (2010).

Americanness (her abundant 'fro), along with Marte Garcia's excellent brown-black color work of her skin, J. Scott Campbell's variant cover art slips into the age-old tradition of hypersexualizing women of color in comics. (See May 2016 *Invincible Iron Man*, vol. 2, #10, as well as *Invincible Iron Man: Ironheart*, vol. 1, 2017.)

In 2006, DC introduces Jaime Reyes as the new Blue Beetle. With Keith Giffen, John Rogers, and Matt Sturges (writers) as well as Ig Guara and Cully Hamner (artists), this Latino is fully fleshed out as a U.S.-Mexico border–dwelling working-class teen. His working-class mother (a nurse) and father (a mechanic) raise him and his sister, Milagro. The adults speak Spanish, and the younger generation code-switches Spanish and English. This is to say, there's a great will to re-create Latinoness on many different levels in the new *Blue Beetle*, including also the visual design of his mask (*luchador*-like) and his battle royal against the *luchador*-like Rompe Huesos. And this re-creation includes nefarious borderland practices, as when Jaime discovers that his Tia Ampero (a.k.a. La Dama) is trafficking in drugs and people, as well as exploiting undocumented Latinos through illegal labor and loan practices.

Through a great will to style present in the writing and the geometrizing of character, this Latinx Blue Beetle makes new our perception, thought, and feeling about the day-to-day existence of living in the U.S.-Mexico borderlands, and the emotional complexity of being a superhero. This is to say, the creators give equal weight to Jaime's characterization as Latino and as superhero. As created equal parts ordinary Latino and superhero alien, he resists assimilation into a superhero identity that loses his Latinoness, making him, in the words of Maurico Espinoza, "even more hybrid and multifaceted" ("The Alien Is Here to Stay: Otherness, Anti-assimilation, and Empowerment in Latino/a Superhero Comics," 188).

Of late, DC has created several minor but interesting Latina superheroes. There is Kurt Busiek, Fabian Nicienza (writers), and Scott McDaniel's (artist) creation of Marguerita "Rita" Covas as Tarot in *Trinity* #3 (June 2008). McDaniel shades her as ethnically Latina. Busiek and Nicienza invest her with prophetic powers, the reading of Tarot cards, that allow her to help her working-class Latino/a community of Mar Vista. On one occasion a character tells Rita, "Hey, Tarot-chica, gracias! I asked for a raise like you said—it worked" ("Earth to Rita," *Trinity* #3, June 2008). The creators are careful not to freeze her in some distant, folkloric past. In spite of her mystical power that might otherwise characterize her as somehow anchored in the past, the creative team portrays her as a young Latina living in the present world. We see this not only in her clothes but also in her accoutrements like her iPod.

Figure 50. Marguerita "Rita" Covas as Tarot in *Trinity* #3 (June 2008).

There are other minor Latina superheroes that arrive on the scene during this period. For instance, Geoff Johns (writer) and Jesús Saiz (artist) introduce Rhonda Pineda as the supervillain Atomica from Earth-3 (*Aquaman*, vol. 7, #16, March 2013). Like her Anglo counterpart, Ray Palmer as Atom, she's invested with the ability to shrink. And, while Saiz hypersexualizes her by accentuating her bosom and putting her in a red spandex one-piece outfit to accentuate her curves, Johns writes her as a highly educated Latina especially adept at hacking computer systems. Interestingly, too, with the characterization of Atomica as having killed children and as a double agent and double-crosser (Crime Syndicate and

Justice League of America) there's an allusion to two Latina figures in Mexican history and myth: *la llorona* and *la malinche*. In one, more heterosexist version of they myth of *la llorona* she drowns her children in revenge for a lover who leaves her for another woman. And, in the heterosexist version of *la malinche*, the historical figure of the Nahua woman Malintzin, who, as the lover of Hernán Cortes, betrayed the Aztecs to the Spaniards. Today, Latinx feminist scholars have excavated the positive, empowering histories of these figures.

And in 2013 Geoff Johns (writer) and Doug Mahnke (artist) create the suburban Latina Jessica Viviana Cruz, the victim of mob violence, as having inherited a power ring and become a new Green Lantern of Earth and member of the Justice League (*Green Lantern*, vol. 5, #20, July 2013). She's trained by Anglo Hal Jordan and fights off an *alien* invasion in Arizona (the ring alerts her to an unauthorized alien presence) only to discover that someone had already used a shotgun to kill the aliens, now piled up in a basement. While Johns and Mahnke do make this new member of the Green Lanterns a Latina, they slip into that tradition of portraying her as in need of a strong male for comfort (Batman or Hal Jordan) and as hypersexualized, with her skintight costume accentuating a big bosom. (See also *Green Lantern, Vol. 1: Rage Planet*, 2017.)

During this period we begin to see a greater will to style exercised in the creating of gay Latino superheroes. Scott Lobdell (writer) and Brett Booth (artist) create Miguel José Barragon as Bunker (*Teen Titans*, vol. 4, #3, January 2012). Bunker complicates and extends the short line of gay Latino superheroes already discussed, especially, of course, his caricatured predecessor Extraño. As Richard T. Rodriguez sums up, "Distinct from Hero Cruz and Living Lightning while more closely aligned with Extraño, Miguel is not cast as hypermasculine but rather quite the opposite" ("Revealing Secret Identities: Gay Latino Superheroes and the Necessity," 232). With Miguel there is no coming out, as seen with Hero Cruz, or any angst about his sexuality, as seen with Fade. Rather, Miguel simply is gay and Latino. With fellow Teen Titan, Wonder Girl, he simply states: "You do realize I'm gay, right?" She responds, "It isn't a big deal, I'm not judging." And, when he comes out to his Mexican family in El Chilar, Mexico, they simply accept him. There's no coming out trauma. There's not a sense that Bunker is gratuitously gay. He's simply gay.

Figure 51. Miguel Barragon with Wonder Girl in *Teen Titans*, vol. 4 "Light and Dark" (2014).

And when Miguel meets up with Anglo fellow teen superhero Red Robin, he does show affection (*cariños*) by giving him a hug, but he also readies for battle against supervillains like Grymm.

In *Teen Titans*, vol. 5, "Home Sweet Home," Booth geometrizes Miguel riding Garfield Logan as Beast Boy, and Lobdell creates a narrator that remarks: "Admittedly they are new friends. But both young men share a passion for life that has bonded them quickly—and perhaps forever." However, these affections are just that—affections, and very much grounded in the Latino cultural tradition of showing affection through hugs and touch. Lobdell creates Bunker as bilingual and Catholic, and in a way that's quite natural. For instance, *Teen Titans*, vol. 5, "The Trial of Kid Flash" (2015), opens with a flashback of Miguel apologizing to God in Spanish: "<I want to apologize for whatever I did that made you so angry. So angry that you allowed Gabriel to go into a coma. [. . .] If I'm not doing your will, heavenly father, then please give me . . . a sign?>" That is, Lobdell and Booth's will to style naturalizes Bunker's queerness and Latinoness. All these interactions are present, in a natural way, and they are ultimately subordinate to the superhero story line: Bunker's ability to use psionic bricks to create material shapes as artillery and protection in battle. That is,

Figure 52. Miguel Barragon hugs Red Robin in *Teen Titans*, vol. 1, "It's Our Right to Fight" (2012).

they create Bunker as a superhero who provides more than just *the* token gay thematic.

This isn't to suggest that Booth and Lobdell assimilate Miguel's identities by making them natural. Indeed, when Miguel returns home to El Chilar to reunite with family and discovers that Gabe has come out of a coma, he kisses Gabe without much ado. Lobdell's narrator remarks: "Modesty forbids showing what happens next" (2). And while many straight readers of the comic were shocked and even angry, ultimately Lobdell and Booth created in Bunker a gay Latino superhero who has grown a tremendous fanbase among

Figure 53. Miguel Barragon reunites with his boyfriend, Gabe, in *Teen Titans*, vol. 4, "Light and Dark" (2014).

LGBTQ and Latino readers. Moreover, with the suggestion in issue 16 that he's only come into *some* of his powers, we may have yet more to see with this story arc. (For more about Bunker's reader reception, see Ricky Rodriguez's "Revealing Secret Identities.")

In 2011, the Marvel universe sees several significant Latinx makeovers, including Blatino Victor Alvarez as Power Man (collected in *Power Man and Iron Fist*, "The Comedy of Death," 2011). Writer Fred Van Lente, along with artists Wellenton Alves and Pere Pérez, creates Victor Alvarez, who embraces his African

Figure 54. Miguel kisses Gabe in *Teen Titans*, vol. 4, "Light and Dark" (2014).

American and Latino identity in a very matter-of-fact way. He likes "fried plantains with queso," collects bullets for his cousin Sofía's jewelry-making business, and has a single mama, Reina Alvarez, who seamlessly switches back and forth between English and Spanish. Vic's father was the Latino supervillain Hernan "Shades" Alvarez, identified by Vic in this as "Specs." Knowing Vic's background, Luke Cage reaches out to him: "We got the same background, you and me. Dad nowhere around—raised just by our moms in this city" (*Power Man and Iron Fist*, "The Comedy of Death"). Vic and fellow Hero for Hire Daniel Rand as Iron Fist fight supervillains like the sombrero-wearing, mustachioed calavera, Don of the Dead, and criollo swashbuckler Alejandro Montoya as El Aguila. However, Lente doesn't play these Latino supervillains straight, infusing a certain playful self-reflexivity into their banter. Readers are meant to laugh at the superior European airs of El Aguila, who refers to himself in the third person and as above street riffraff like Iron Fist and Power Man: "No, no, no. El Aguila will not duel any man with such a pedestrian cognomen," he tells Iron Man (*Power Man and Iron Fist*, "The Comedy of Death"). And, Lent, Alves, and Pérez provide a panoply of racist neo-Nazi and white trash thugs as counterpoints to these Latinos.

In *Mighty Avengers, Vol. 1: No Single Hero* (2014) Power Man reappears with former classmate Ava Ayala as White Tiger (along with Luke Cage, Spider-Man, Spectrum, Dr. Strange, and others)

Figure 55. Neo-Nazi thugs in *Power Man and Iron First*, "The Comedy of Death" (2011).

in a city filled to the brim with Spanish- and English-speaking Latinos. To defeat the ultimate threat to humanity, Deathwalker Prime, writer Al Ewing and artist Greg Land pair up White Tiger and Power Man as a unified multiethnic superpower: "We are matter and antimatter. Science and magic. Male and female. We are the secret song of birds and the spirit within all things. We are gods ancient and unborn. We are The Avenger Prime" (*Mighty Avengers, Vol. 3: Original Sin*). Ewing and Land depict the power of Latino unity in action.

In 2011 we saw another important Marvel Latino/a makeover. Rob Williams (writer), Matthew Clark, Brian Ching, Lee Garbett, Sean Parsons, and Rob Schwager (artists) create Alejandra "Angela" as the latest incarnation of Bronze Age creation Johnny Blaze as Ghost Rider (*Ghost Rider: Fear Itself*, vol. 7, #1). In a tie-in volume, *Fear Itself: Ghost Rider*, to a seven-issue crossover (April–October 2011) series, writer Williams with artist Matthew Clark et al. create nineteen-year-old Angela, orphaned daughter of a human trafficker and an unknown Mexican woman who the Seeker chooses to inhabit and make into the new Ghost Rider.

Immune to pain and injury, as well as able to project fire from her eyes, hands, and mouth, Angela learns to control and shape the fire, using it as a weapon (scythe), protection (walls of hellfire), and a mode of transportation (motorcycle). She is sent on several missions, including to Dayton, Ohio, to fight Skadi, the daughter of the Red Skull, and later to Las Vegas to stop Mephisto's son, Blackheart, from bringing hell to earth via a portal.

And, as part of the reboot with the Marvel Now! titles, Ghost Rider returns as the Latino Robbie Reyes in the *All-New Ghost Rider* Earth-616 series (2014–). Blatino (Jamaican/Argentinean American) creator Felipe Smith (writer) and African Americans Damion Scott (artist) and Tradd Moore (artist for vol. 2, *Engines of Vengeance*) team up to fully flesh out Ghost Rider *as* Latino and as *of his Latino community*. In an interview with David Betancourt, Smith comments on growing up in a family where diversity was the norm and the importance of writing Latino culture into the story ("'All-New Ghost Rider': Creative Muscle to the Reborn Spirit of Vengeance"). The creative team invents Reyes as a high school student who is trying to make ends meet as a mechanic while raising his differently abled younger brother, Gabriel, a victim of bullying.

Figure 56. Alejandra "Angela" as Ghost Rider in *Ghost Rider: Fear Itself*, vol. 7, #1 (August 2011).

In the writing and the visuals, the creative team develops his character in the fully realized Latino community of East L.A. ("Hillock Heights"), filled with all types of Latinos.

As the story unfolds, Robbie not only subdues the bad guys, including the well-known Marvel supervillain Calvin Zabo as Mr. Hyde, but brings order to an otherwise cartel-run, fearful neighborhood. In a slight shift from earlier Ghost Rider plots, Robbie is possessed by the spirit of his late uncle, Eli Morrow, and is not an incarnation of Johnny Blazes. The tension: to exact revenge and bring order to the neighborhood means allowing the sociopathic Morrow to possess him more and more, to the point that he neglects his duties as older brother and caretaker to Gabe.

Figure 57. Robbie Reyes defends his disabled brother, Gabe, in *All-New Ghost Rider* #1 (March 2014).

During this same contemporary period we also see Marvel give Spider-Man a Latino—Afrolatino—makeover. In Marvel's Ultimate Comics series, Michael Bendis (writer) and Sara Pichelli (artist) introduce Brooklyn-born-and-raised teen Miles Morales (*Ultimate Fallout* #4, August 2011) as the black, red-webbed Spider-Man, replete with a red spider logo outfit. In this parallel universe, Peter Parker dies (at the hands of the Green Goblin) and a genetically modified spider bites Morales (courtesy of Oscorp). Miles is a super smart teenager living in an apartment with his loving Nuyorican mama, Rio, and his morally rigid African American father, Jefferson Davis. When Miles's grades at school start slipping because of his superhero work, Bendis and Pichelli introduce Miles's strong-spirited, bilingual *abuela*, Gloria Morales.

Bendis and Pichelli's willful distillation and reconstruction of our contemporary multicultural U.S. reality continue to fill out the story, creating the Asian American character Ganke Lee as Miles's best friend and confidant. (Notably, in John Watts's 2017 film re-creation, *Spider-Man: Home Coming*, the Asian sidekick is the only multicultural character; Blatino Spidey is passed over for Anglo actor Tom Holland.) While Miles's mixed-race roots are made clear, in the end Bendis and Pichelli still create a superhero

Figure 58. Miles is scolded by a tough *abuelita* in *Spider-Man*, vol. 2, #2 (May 2016).

storyworld. They create a character who experiences psychological ups and downs with his mixed-race identity and web kinship ties *and* as a superhero. At one point he battles his own uncle, Aaron Davis as the supervillain Prowler, who works for the Mexican crime lord Scorpion. And, in a battle royale with African American Dr. Conrad Marcus as Venom, Miles watches his mother, Rio, die. She is fatally wounded by Venom and shot in the police cross fire. Bendis and Pichelli powerfully create this scene of loss and true revelation. Rio realizes Miles is Spider-Man but asks that he keep this from his father.

Miles comes clean to his father (who leaves him—as it turns out, he's an agent of S.H.I.E.L.D.), only to discover that the original Anglo Peter Parker is alive—resuscitated from the grave. The tension introduced here: Norman Osborne reveals that he's Miles's true father, and Parker suffers from a sort of doppelgänger syndrome, wondering if he's a clone or not: "I remember my entire life and I remember my death" (Bendis with artist David Marquez in *Miles Morales: The Ultimate Spider-Man*, vol. 2, "Revelations"). Parker goes on a quest to find himself, gifts his web shooters to Miles, then tells him: "You be Spider-Man. My blessing. It's all yours."

In 2013, both DC and Marvel resuscitate Latino superheroes from yesteryear and also give Latino makeovers to Anglo superheroes. For instance, Marvel's Kieron Gillen (writer) and Jaime McKelvie (artist) introduce LGBTQ America Chavez as a steady, new member to their new Young Avengers team (*Young Avengers* #1, January 2013); she debuts in Joe Casey (writer) and Nick Dragotta's (artist) 2011 limited series, *Vengeance* (#1, July 2011). We discover that bilingual America is a runaway living in New York City (Earth-616), raised by two mothers on the planet Utopia in the Utopian Parallel; the mothers sacrifice themselves to save Utopia from being sucked into the multiverse. America has superhuman strength, the ability to fly, and the ability to move at super speeds, passing between Earth-212 and Earth-616, for instance; she's also bulletproof and flame retardant. She's recruited by a fellow teen, Loki, to join the new Young Avengers; this is a team put together (see Allan Heinberg and Jim Cheung, #1, April 2005) in antici-pation of the disbanding of the Avengers; and while the Young

Figure 59. Miles loses his Nuyorican mama in *Ultimate Comics Spider-Man*, vol. 2, #22 (June 2013).

Avengers model themselves on the older ones, the Avengers refuse to train them without parental consent. During the first issues of the new Young Avengers, Loki says that America has anger issues; as it turns out, while he might identify her as the stereotypical hot-headed Latina, Gillen and McKelvie create a more complex char-acter. She gets angry, but not without reason. She resorts to anger and violence when the other Young Avengers are too slow to get the job done, or when she's pushed to her own limits by the likes of a bratty young Loki. That is, Gillen and McKelvie create her not as a hothead but as a Latina superhero driven to right wrongs and take supervillains—and without the usual spandex. And, along the way she seeks to become her own person as a Latina and lesbian. When Kate Bishop takes pause and asks, "Wait—Hold up! Am I the only person on the team who's straight?" America responds: "Princess. I've seen the way you look at me. You're not that straight" (*Young Avengers*, vol. 2, #15).

Figure 60. America Chavez responds to Kate Bishop in *Young Avengers*, vol. 2, #15 (March 2014).

In 2013, DC resuscitates Vibe as part of the New 52 reboot. He lives again in *Justice League of America's Vibe* #1 (February 2013). Andrew Kreisberg (writer) and Pete Woods (artist) swap out "Paco" for "Cisco," his nickname, derived from Francisco Ramon. When Cisco is exposed to interdimensional forces that reconfigure his DNA and give him vibratory superpowers, he loses his brother Armando to another dimension; Armando returns as the brainwashed supervillain Rupture. Kreisberg and Woods fully develop Cisco's character within close-knit Latino family life in a richly textured urban Detroit environment. As the story unfolds, so, too, do the readers get a sense of Cisco as Vibe's development as a character—not just in the discovery of the absolute limits of his superpowers, but also as a young Latino male making ends meet with his brother, Dante, and single-parent papa in an apartment in Detroit.

Figure 61. Cisco returns home to single-parent papa in *Justice League of America's Vibe* #1 (February 2013).

Kreisberg and Woods re-create him as a compelling Latino superhero, not just in terms of characterization and plot, but also in Woods's kinetic drawing. Unfortunately, the writing and geometrizing of Vibe in the *New 52 Justice League of America*, vol. 3, #2 (May 2013) leaves his Latino complexity behind—as well as his kinetic visual portrayal. It's the same Latino superhero, but he generates absolutely no interest because of the writing and especially the drawing.

○○○

As I wrap up this chapter, I want to mention a few additional Marvel and DC Latino supervillains not discussed thus far. While these are not A-listers like Apocalypse, Osborn/Green Goblin, Doctor Octopus, Magneto, Lex Luthor, The Joker, and Bizarro, DC and Marvel do create a handful of interesting antagonists. Marvel introduces two significant Latino supervillains: Antonio Rodriguez as Armadillo (*Captain America*, "Armadillo!" #308, August 1985) and Robert Velasquez as Bantam (*Captain America Annual* #12, 1993). And DC creates Cadre, Anton Allegro, Scorpion, and Amazon. Also, DC introduces a memorable Latina supervillain when Len Wein (writer), along with Chuck Patton and Dell

Figure 62. A static Vibe in *Justice League of America*, vol. 3, #2 (May 2013).

Barras (artists), creates Amelinda Lopez as the witty, street-smart, leotard-wearing, metal alloy (promethium)–infused, and super muscled Touch-N-Go (*Blue Beetle*, vol. 1, #10, March 1987).

Notably, too, in the twenty-first century we begin to see more Latino characters fill out storyworlds as secondary and tertiary characters, to make for a more representative multicultural setting. For instance, in DC's *Wonder Woman* series (2003–) Greg Rucka (writer) and Cliff Richards and Ray Snyder (artists) include on Wonder Woman's staff Alana Dominguez. In DC's Greg Rucka and Michael Lark's *Gotham Central*, Daria Hernandez is introduced as a pastry chef by profession and lover of GCPD homicide detective Renée Montoya; she supports Renée when she's outed in the department and rejected by her family, but later leaves her when Renée turns to drink. Also in the DC universe Judd Winick and Guillem March (artists) feature Carlos Alvarez as the police detective of Gotham City in *Catwoman* (2012–).

As I end this chapter, which focuses on Latino representations in mainstream print comic book storyworlds, I hope I have excavated an archive of Latino superhero (and supervillain) representation in mainstream comics. I also hope to have begun to identify comics that demonstrate a greater or lesser degree of a will to style in their distillation and reconstruction of a reality where Latinos have become the majority minority *and* in the geometrizing of form in these re-creations of Latinos.

Certainly, as this brief history shows, DC and Marvel have made some whoppers. But they've also created comics that demonstrate a great degree of a will to style. Such comics distill and reconstruct the world we inhabit in ways that deepen our engagement with this world we live in. And we've seen how this will to style in aesthetics—the geometrizing of the story—makes for some compelling and complex character creation. In these comics we see the creation of storyworlds with imaginative safe spaces for the most vulnerable—those at the margins of society in terms of race, gender, and sexuality. From the 1940s and the horrors of the Holocaust, and the McCarthy era of the 1950s, through the civil rights era to today's intensification of the class divide (the 99% vs. the 1%), we see the creation of Latinos with greater or lesser degrees of will to style concerning content and form. The next chapter begins to articulate a theory of *how* Latinx superhero comic book storyworlds can be built in ways that make *new* our perception, thought, and feeling about fictional and real Latinos.

Chapter 2

TOWARD A THEORY OF LATINX COMIC BOOK SUPERHEROES

Crafty Co-creators

In the last chapter, I presented a sweeping overview of the history of Latinos in the DC and Marvel universes. While a recovery of the brown superhero archive was the main impulse, it necessarily includes an interpretive and evaluative dimension that attends to both the writing and the geometrizing of Latinx superheroes. Indeed, in some we see a great will to style in their creation, and in others less so. This chapter fleshes out more just how the writing and the visuals work to create storyworlds with Latinx superheroes that engage and intensify the reading and viewing experience.

As the last chapter makes clear, the history of Latinos in mainstream comic books is a living, breathing archive that reflects just how we as a Latino population in the United States have changed: from a largely rural minority to an urban majority minority. With our growing demographic presence we see the transformation of everyday U.S. reality. This is to say that today it is much harder for DC and Marvel to ignore us; it takes a willful act on the part of creators *not* to include Latinos in comics. As our presence has grown, so, too, have DC and Marvel come to see us as potential readers and, therefore, as potential *buyers* of comics. And guess what: we do like reading comics of all kinds, including those that represent us within their pages. We enjoy that perceptual, cognitive, and emotive engagement with comics where there's a strong will to style. We enjoy the process of *co-creating* (with the respective writers and artists) the sights, sounds, tastes, smells, touch, movement, thoughts, and feelings of Latino superheroes (and supervillains) we encounter.

To reiterate, co-creating is the mental process involved in the audience's apprehension then emotion and cognitive meaning making of the comic book storyworld. Indeed, it is the wonderfully generative capacity of this co-creating potential in comic book readers that not only allows readers and audiences to imagine movement and three dimensions in the static, two-dimensional in-print comic book storyworld spaces, but also allows them to feel and think about identities and experiences distant from their own. It's this capacity that allows Latinos to imagine beyond the boundaries of Anglo superhero comics; even if Batman doesn't look like us, we can imagine ourselves as Batman. It's this generative mental capacity that allows non-Latino creators to exercise their willfulness in reconstructing Latino experiences and identities in complex and meaningful ways.

Our *co-creative* engagement with comic books that feature Latinos is nuanced and complex. When I step into the shoes of the hypersexualized Roberto da Costa as Sunspot, I don't begin to think of myself as an oversexed Latino. Instead I ask: is this characteristic well integrated into his psychology, or is it a token appendage? That is, do the parts make up an integrated whole, and, if so, how might this enhance my engagement with da Costa as a fictional reconstruction of a select number of experiences, traits, and behaviors that inform Latino subjectivity?

When we open a comic and begin to read and view its pages, we *co-create*. The authors and artists select in *and* out details (writing and visuals) that at once hit our perception system *and* guide our imagination to thrill in their filling in of gaps; our emotions and thoughts fill in and complete drawn figures, gestures, dialogue, and character interaction, for instance. When we fill in the gaps, we co-create and we make the story our own. We don't change the story; we follow the carefully selected visual and verbal cues that make up the blueprint to *co-create* the story. We become chiasmic transformers, all while not changing the DNA of the story itself.

Mainstream comic book creators can and do distill products from reality (intellectual and material) in order to create (reorganize, and rebuild) comic books with Latinos as their subjects. Since the 1970s, and especially of late, creators (teams of writers, pencilers, inkers, and editors) have increasingly distilled, then reconstructed, comic book storyworlds based on building blocks of a U.S. reality thick with Latinos. Given that our reality is increasingly a Latino American reality, when we don't see Latinos in these storyworlds, it's less a careless slip and more a willful (shameful) erasure. (As I'll discuss in chapter 3, this is even more apparent in animation, TV shows, and films.) This said, it is also important to keep in mind that when these creators reconstruct a U.S. reality that's increasingly Latino, what they make is not a carbon copy of this reality. It is the map, and not *the territory*. It is a distillation and reconstruction of U.S. reality through verbal and visual means that guide our filling in of gaps; that guide our co-creation of storyworlds with Latino superheroes. To put it more technically, DC and Marvel creators make visual and verbal blueprints that ask readers to exercise their causal, counterfactual, and probabilistic mechanisms not only to *re-create* social and physical maps of their respective storyworlds, but also to *imagine* new possible ways of existing in the real world. As Adilifu Nama discusses in *Super Black*, some black superheroes reinforce racist stereotypes, and others challenge "calcified notions of blackness as a racial category and source of cultural meaning" (*Super Black*, 5–6). For Nama, when there's a great willfulness present in the creation of a black superhero, then, in so many words, it invites the reader into this more active and transformative co-creative space. Superhero comics that feature otherwise racially marginalized subjects and that are created with a great degree of a will to style to actively trigger this co-creative process not only can lead to the possibility of opening our eyes to racism in the world, but, according to Nama, can also offer a vision of what a positive, racially inclusive society can become tomorrow. (See, too, Jason Dittmer's *Captain America and the Nationalist Superhero*, where he identifies how DC and Marvel superhero comics can offer ways for readers to reimagine and reconsider ideologies of U.S. exceptionalism.)

This said, it's also important to keep in mind that we, as readers, are not passive, absorptive sponges. Clearly, I'm on the side that defends the willful creation of comics where the writing and the visuals make for an exciting experience. When Brian Michael Bendis (writer) and Sara Pichelli (artist) choose to re-create Spider-Man as the Puerto Rican/Black Miles Morales, they bring to it a willfulness (writing, visuals, and whatever research might be required) that engages fully our co-creative processes as Latino and African American readers; they invite us to fully co-create ourselves as Spider-Man. However, it also invites non-Latinos and non-African American readers to co-create themselves as a teen, male Blatino Spider-Man. My ten-year-old daughter, Corina, identifies as Mexipina, yet she can and does delight in imagining herself as a mixed-race Puerto Rican and African American teen wall crawler and web spinner. Such a comic does establish story lines and a fixity of character (what's written and drawn on the page today will be the same tomorrow) that direct her gap-filling capacities, but where she *goes* in her gap-filling—her imagination—is not predetermined. Through the cognitive processes involved in co-creation, Corina can and *does* go beyond the comic book's storyworld design and delineation.

I mention my daughter, but this is what happens with all of us when we engage with comic books. Latino comic book creators, such as George Pérez, talk about their own early experiences as *co-creating* (my words, of course) when reading comics. Pérez imagined himself as Batman (*Brace and the Bold*) and any number of those from the *Fantastic Four*; that they were Anglo characters made no difference to the five-year-old monolingual Spanish-speaking Pérez growing up in a tenement in the Bronx. (See Lawrence, *Storyteller*.) Other, more recent generations of Latinx author/artists, like Ivan Velez Jr. (*Blood Syndicate*), similarly remark on this *co-creative* experience. *Archie, Richie Rich, Superman, Supergirl* didn't feature Bronx-born-and-raised Nuyorican characters, yet Velez Jr.'s co-creative capacity allowed him to step into their shoes and slide into their capes in emancipatory ways. It was his way of imagining himself beyond the limitations of a queerphobic and racist world. (See *Your Brain on Latino Comics*.) And for the young Frank Espinosa (*Rocketo*), living in Cuba before migrating to the United States, The Phantom, Mandrake the Magician, and Popeye "opened up a whole new world" (*Your Brain on Latino Comics*, 152). Espinosa looked past Superman's white skin and European features to imagine himself to be a superhero who could overcome the racism experienced as an outsider (alien) in another land (United States). And when Chicano comic book creator Javier Hernandez (*El Muerto*) was a youngster, he was able to imagine himself as the Anglo Peter Parker because he was a nerd who had problems "getting the girls," working for "a boss that's always chewing him out," and who "never has money" (*Your Brain on Latino Comics*, 196). Chicana comic book author Laura Molina couldn't get enough of the DC and Marvel comics, even though they did not feature Latina superheroes, because they allowed her to *imagine* herself as empowered to do good for the community. I, myself, recall vividly stepping into the shoes of Superman, Batman, and Mexican *luchadores*, and all at once. There wasn't any direct correlation between my identity and experience as a mixed Mexican, Guatemalan, Irish Latino living in California, yet they made me feel like the sky wasn't even the limit. Due to the wondrous plasticity of the mind and its expansive imaginative functions, we *co-create* from that which is least like us, and in ways that can be empowering.

To sum up: we as readers of comic book storyworlds that feature superheroes (Latinx and all others) are at once anchored to the textual and visual design of the comic (the blueprint, say), but, because of our capacity for active *co-creation*, we are not bound to it in determinative ways. We aren't sponges that passively absorb superheroes that don't look or act like us. Maybe the superhero is older, white, straight, and male. This doesn't mean that those of us who don't identify within these categories can't *co-create* such a figure as our own. As our attention moves back and forth between the reading elements (verbal) and the drawn elements (visual), we perceive, interpret, and feel in a loosely guided way; and in so doing we fill in the gaps with our own experiences and identities. We make it our own. This is to reiterate that, while clearly we want to promote the making of engaging comics that are, thus, inclusive of complex and various Latinx superheroes, even those that don't do this still leave room for our imagination to fill in gaps with our own individual and idiosyncratic experiences, memories, and emotions.

Crafty Geometric Shapers

DC and Marvel superhero storyworlds rely heavily on the geometrizing of story as the dominant element at play in our co-creating activities. It is the skillful and willful visualizing—*geometrizing*—of character, theme, and plot that guides our gap-filling processes and shapes our experience of a given comic book. It's the visuals that primarily drive our co-creative insertion into a storyworld.

The building of and giving visual shape to the comic book storyworld that feature Latino superheroes begins with the artists.

These characters are brought to life by those pencilers, inkers, and colorists who have spent (and continue to spend) nearly all their waking, breathing lives practicing and sharpening their visual-shaping-device skills. Part of this training includes a given artist's mastery and then going beyond the visual artistry of innovative artists who've caught his or her attention. I think here of Jaime and Gilbert Hernandez, who spent much of their childhood and teens mastering, then exploring and making their own the work of Harry Lucey (*Archie*) and Jack Kirby, among others. It was Kirby's incredible ability to create the "powerful sense of these characters flying off the page" that inspired Javier Hernandez to become a comic book author/artist (*Your Brain on Latino Comics*, 192). I think also of Rafael Navarro and Rhode Montijo, who were inspired by Steve Ditko, Gene Colan, John Buscema, John Romita Sr., Frank Robbins, Jim Steranko, and Mike Mignola. (See *Your Brain on Latino Comics* and *Latinx Comic Book Storytelling*.) Indeed, one of the most notable Latinos working squarely within the superhero comic book universe, George Pérez, transformed his art—"muddled by inaccurate anatomy and nearly non-existent perspective" (Lawrence, *Storyteller*, 22)—into something extraordinary under Marv Wolfman's guidance. He became a successful visual creator because Wolfman pushed him to perfect the art of *geometrizing* the story. With slightly different details, we see this story repeat itself with the many other Latino artists who work for DC and Marvel today. (See Appendix.) In each case, the artist learned how to *geometrize* comic book stories by first mastering the techniques of their predecessors, and then taking these innovations in new directions to give energy and life to storytelling.

The geometric shaping of the story is one of the two main subsystems that make up comic book storytelling. The other is the verbal subsystem (narrator boxes, dialogue, and thoughts of characters, for instance). However, the visual subsystem in superhero comics is dominant. It gives shape to character and action *in* time and *across* different spaces of the storyworld. The shape, color, and posture guide how we *make sense* of the character; how we understand the character *to be* in the world. And the geometrizing of other elements of the storyworld, such as the written text, can allow us to experience their physicality. We hear a *SWOOSH* as well as the bellyache of the *POW!* and *KA-BLAMMM!*

Jack Kirby's great contribution to comics was his geometrizing of story. In *Hands of Fire* Charles Hatfield writes how Kirby was the "master of impatient, explosive, hyperkinetic action comics" (8). For Hatfield, Kirby embodies the "graphic storyteller" par excellence through his creation of visual narratives that burst with energy. Kirby, he continues, "treats bodies as bodies in time or vectors of force, as well as abstract design elements"(45). Kirby's geometrizing of the story—and for Hatfield this is especially the case with *Thor* (1962–1970) and *The Fantastic Four* (1961–1970)—showed comic book creators just how powerful the visuals could be in generating sophisticated, kinetic comic book storyworlds. He showed generations of narrative artists that careful *geometrizing* of story actively shapes how audiences engage with and make sense of the storyworld. Kirby showed generations of comic book creators how the will to *geometrize* the story can and does generate storyworlds in ways that amplify, enlarge, and *make new* our perception, thought, and feeling about the world we live in.

All the superhero comics that I discussed in earlier sections of the book are variously a compendium of tools and forms found in other visual dominant art forms, like painting, film, TV—even video games. In each case we see how teams of artists use the tools of the visual arts in all their guises to re-create those building blocks taken from reality; they *re*construct these building blocks in their particularized assemblage of geometric forms. They *geometrize* the story (the textual/verbal shaping of plot, theme, character) with the use of the visual shaping devices.

The geometrizing of the building blocks of reality are taken from all that makes up the world—including art itself as grown from the natural, inherent way we as homo faber have cultivated since infancy and childhood our perception system to recognize depth, width, and height—and give weight to objects in our everyday activities. In *How to Draw Comics* Stan Lee considers how "most things around you are based on three essential geometric shapes: the circle (or sphere), the square (or cube), and the cylinder. Even a human being!" (36). That is, he identifies how the growing of our everyday perceptual encounter with the world can be sharply focused when artists choose to spend time perfecting the creating of 2D shapes that can be experienced as three-dimensional storyworlds. In other words, the skillful use of geometric shapes (circles, triangles, and rectangles), along with perspective (adding a sense of weight and volume, for instance), can turn 2D lines on a page into a 3D *experience* in our minds.

This is to say, and as already gestured toward in chapter 1, the choice of shape, line, perspective (and ink and color) plays a significant role in determining whether readers experience any given Latinx superhero as complex; the choice of geometric shape (and perspective) used for, say, a nose, a set of lips, or the size and shape of a head can and does convey complexity in our experience of a Latinx superhero.

The geometrizing of the story doesn't end with shapes given to figures. There are the shapes given to the panels and their layout that guide the pacing of the story proper (and our reading) and our meaning-making processes. Whether a three-panels-wide-by-six-panels-tall layout or a splash-page (and this is only to mention some of the infinite possibilities), visuals created in the specific sequencing of panels tell us much about the storyworld and its characters. As Mark Ellis and Melissa Martin Ellis sum up, to be a great comic book storyteller one "must understand character design, perspective, proportion, light and dark values, and, perhaps most importantly, how to tell a story in a sequence of images" (*The Everything Guide to Writing Graphic Novels*, 62).

Comic book storytellers know well the significance of the visuals. And I'm certainly not the first, say, theorist to pay attention to this. I think readily of the theories proposed by Jan Baetens, Karin Kukonnen, Pascal Lefèvre, and Jared Gardner, who focus their attention on creating a conceptual vocabulary for identifying how the different visual devices work to give shape to comic book storyworlds. For Baetens, the choice of how the artists determine the pattern of the "montage of images of panels" provides not only a "visual rhythm" but an interpretive framework that guides our abstraction processes ("Abstractions in Comics," 95). Kukonnen considers that the drawings from one panel to another can create a simultaneous experience of layers of space and time (flashbacks, flash forwards, and the quick move between simultaneously occurring events in different places) in ways that one can't do with alphabetic storytelling, which relies on our sequencing from left to right (or right to left) in time. (See Kukonnen, "Comics as a Test Case for Transmedial Narratology.") Pascal Lefèvre teases out not only nuances of how the panel can open up the "spatio-temporal" possibilities of comic book storytelling, but also how the panel sequencing and layout can convey "a particular visual ontology [that suggests] to the reader a particular way of interpreting the storyworld" (31). For Lefèvre, panel layout and speech balloon placement are crucial elements that *educate* readers in how to make sense of the time and space of the story. They function as spatial signposts that guide how readers move their eyes and attention across and down the page. Their placement can determine the pace, tempo, and rhythm of the reading/viewing experience. The visual shaping devices of the gutter and the drawn line itself are the essence of comics for Jared Gardner. For Gardner, the accumulation of drawn lines is its "diction and syntax" ("Storylines," 57). Whether thin or thick, jagged or wavy, circular, triangular, and so on, for Gardner it's the accumulation of lines that determines a comic book's style, mood, and worldview.

What I emphasize here is that with superhero comics a will to *geometrize* the story is paramount. Superhero comics rely on developing characters and events through motion and movement. If there's no energy in the geometrizing of the storyworld, there's no kinesis of consciousness. Put simply, if there is a diminished will to *geometrize* the story in the making of superhero comic books that feature Latinos, the character and plot suffer.

Geometric Storytelling *in Action*

The geometrizing of the story is the heart of this storytelling art. Of course, in the DC and Marvel industries this is not the product of one artist, but many—and often many different sets of artists as one moves from one issue to the next within the same comic book series. Today, many such artists (pencilers, inkers, and colorists) are Latino. (See Appendix.) In fact, as I've been discussing all along here, given the significant role played by the art, they are arguably the most important part of comic book creation in the DC and Marvel marketplace. While the plots are important, they tend to be variants of the same: origin, education, superheroic action with its conflicts and resolutions. Where we see the real innovation is in the way the plots are geometrized. This is to say, the Latino artists are arguably the true innovators. They are our modern-day Renaissance creators. For instance, it's Javier Rodríguez's coloring on *Young Avengers*, David Marquez's art for *Ultimate Comics Spider-Man*, Marte Garcia's lettering for *Nova*, Jaime Mendoza's inking on *Heroes for Hire* and *X-Factor*, Victor Olazaba's inking for *Araña* and *X-Men*, Roger Cruz's artwork on *Ghost Rider*, Rafael Albuquerque's and Ig Guara's artwork on *Blue Beetle*, and Edgar Delgado's art for *Spider-Girl: Family Values* that make the Latino superheroes pop with vitality. Pencilers like Alvaro Rio and Humberto Ramos, working on *White Tiger*, not only create all that goes into the visuals of the storyworld, but they also keep centrally in mind all the continuity details that make the visual characterization of the new White Tiger coherently *in character* so that we invest our thought and emotion in the story. As Olazaba inks the lines of those penciled drawings of *Araña*, he makes important decisions about line thickness to convey a unique style and, with this, a mood and worldview. When Javier Rodriguez colors *Young Avengers*, he makes certain interpretations of the inked drawings to decide not only which colors he'll use to identify a Latino character, but also which colors (light or dark) to use to intensify mood. The choice of shape and size of letters by someone like Marte Garcia alerts us to how we are supposed to emotionally experience Sam Alexander's thoughts and dialogue as the Latino new Nova.

While here I separate out each of these visual ingredients involved in shaping superhero comic book storyworlds that feature Latinos, in the end the visuals work together as a gestaltic whole. This gestaltic experience happens even before we open the comic to its first page. It happens in our total apprehension of the cover. Covers are our first encounter with a comic book (and possibly a series). As a first contact, they can entice us (or not) to open and scan, then own or borrow the comic for a good read and reread. The carefully wrought cover gives a snapshot of the contents; it's a kind of flash-fiction gestalt of the characters encountered, action delivered, and mood cultivated. For instance, Cully Hamner's cover for DC's *The Question: Pipeline* (2011) clearly identifies the protagonist in the right foreground (Renee

Montoya with her faceless mask as The Question): she's fisted up, twisted, slightly ready to spring to action.

Figure 63. Cover of *The Question: Pipeline* (2011).

In the background, with a red color wash other key players appear in terms of hierarchy of importance: the close-up of Aristotle "Tot" Rodor is slightly more in the foreground than the masked portrait of The Huntress; flames also appear. The contrastive colors and inked lines give a dynamism to the cover with *The Question: Pipeline* running at a slight angle across the top of the page.

Glenn Fabry's cover for *Batman: Vengeance of Bane* #1 (January 1993) features the muscled, masked Bane bent over three drooped dead guards (prison) positioned in a triangular shape at his feet. A close-up of Batman in side view appears in the background. His angry look is tinged with sadness; what little of his face we see deliberately makes him look tired—older (wrinkled). The lines of the drawn bodies and shapes move the eye from top (where the title appears) to middle (Bane) to bottom (the guards).

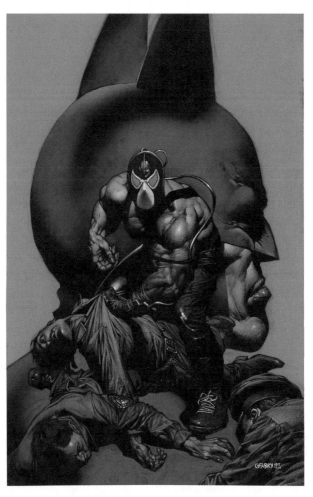

Figure 64. Cover of *Batman: Vengeance of Bane #1* (January 1993).

As with Hamner's *The Question*, so, too, do we see with Fabry's *Batman* how the visuals *shape* a summary of the total contents of the story. In both cases we see how visuals capture the storyworld contents in a gestaltic flash. Moreover, in addition to providing a summary of the content, their respective covers actually *add* to the comic book itself. They supply something additional to a summary. Their cover art intensifies the experience of the comic as an aesthetic whole.

As we move from cover and other paratextual materials into the comic book storyworld proper, we see how the visual devices work to complicate spatial, temporal, and action ingredients in ways that dynamically move the story forward. The artists determine the sequences of panels, placement of splash pages, layout, and spreads. That is, not only do they give shape to how we think and feel when reading a comic, but they also determine the pace of movement between panels and between sequences of panels, and movement within the panels. For instance, in *Araña: Night of the Hunter*, Roger Cruz and Frances Portela choose to use various frames (conventional comic book panels and a gilded picture frame) to telescope us from Anya in the present moment as a teen to her as a young girl. The careful use of visuals and frames within frames indicates our move from present to proximate, then distant, past and between different spaces, including those that signify comfort and life (her childhood home) and death and tragedy (her mother's grave at a cemetery).

While each comic guides (and, with the radically innovative, newly educates) its reader in how to make meaning of its unique shaping of time and space, there are identifiable conventions that we find used across the board in mainstream comics. In fact, we find these as giving shape to film stories, too. They include the use of visuals to situate the action and to create specific consonant and dissonant effects when juxtaposing disparate times and spaces between panels, for instance. When we open to the first pages of *The Question: Pipeline*, for example, the first panel situates us within the story with a long shot, angled from below and tilted to the side that portrays a lighthouse. The narrator box provides further nuance, alerting us to the specifics of geographic location: the Outer Banks of North Carolina. Yet, after this rather conventional opening, there's the juxtaposition of panels that introduce

Montoya training in her sweats and talking with her sidekick, Tort, with a differently colored, medium shot of Montoya dressed as The Question in a different time and place. The visuals allow for such a juxtaposition of disparate times and places, disrupting conventions of continuity that we might expect when a mainstream comic book story begins. However, the artist's skillful use of visual parallelism links these otherwise disparate spatiotemporal moments in our minds. We connect Renee's actions with The Question's movement in space and time. We understand that we are supposed to read the comic along two parallel levels: Renee in the present, but a present that is shared with another time/place (the future?), that of The Question's sleuthing out of global organized crime. The careful organization of the interplay of the visuals allows the comic to launch the story on these two time/space continua that give our gap-filling and sense-making processes a workout—and tremendous satisfaction once we figure out how to read the comic along these two planes. Of course, once Renee becomes The Question, these disparate times and spaces collapse into one.

Figure 65. *Batwoman: Hydrology*, vol. 1 (2012).

Giving shape to the paratextual materials like the title and credit page that follow the cover is hugely important, too, for introducing overarching themes and moods. For instance, J. H. Williams's web of angled line art in the two-page title and credit page for *Batwoman: Hydrology*, vol. 1 (2012) introduces the theme of chaos and confusion (in plot and visuals) that permeates the storyworld proper. It prepares readers for a story that includes Batwoman *and* the mythical Latina La Llorona and that moves forward visually through the juxtaposition of panels depicting disparate time-spaces.

Most of the superhero comics that I discuss in chapter 1 that feature Latino superheroes use visual editing in the paratextual front matter and storyworld proper in more conventional ways, making it easier for our brains to stitch together the time-spaces of each of the panels. One of the ways the artists do this is to create match cuts to identify a scene change in which the last shot of one scene and the first shot of the next scene are similar in composition. They also use cross cutting to allow us to stitch together two or more story lines. They use eye-line matches (and shot-reverse-shot) to create a consistent point of view that guides our sense making as we move from one panel to another and from one shot to another. They tend to lay out the panels individually and in sequence in ways that create a convention for viewing. They use splash pages for us to take pause and relish and absorb the intensity of a moment. They decide the size and shape of the panels in traditional grid layouts. I mention these conventions as, well, conventions because when we come across something like *Batman: Hydrology*, with its radical push against convention, it makes *new* our perception, thought, and feeling about what we are reading.

Using the visual devices to make new our experience of comics with Latinx superheroes doesn't have to be as radical as that seen in *Hydrology*. Consider Pete Woods (penciler), Sean Parsons (inker), and Brad Anderson's (colorist) artwork and layout in the opening page of the New 52's *Justice League of America's Vibe* #1 (February 2013). The visuals in the first panel (stretched across the top of the page) locate us in the time and place of the story: long shot (at slight angle looking down) of a desolate urban cityscape (graffiti on wall) of Detroit (newspaper stand: "Detroit Press") with three figures walking and one kicking a soccer ball. The geometric forms (angled lines of the sidewalk, road, and buildings) give shape and substance to their location; they are situated in an environment with gravity and air to breathe. (The dialogue gives further definition to the characters: the older brother tells his two younger brothers that he will

Figure 66. Opening to *Justice League of America's Vibe* #1 (February 2013).

be leaving for college in California on a football scholarship.) The size of the four following panels (two stretched across the page, then two side by side) builds a rhythmic suspense that lands us on the final stretch panel at the bottom: a medium long shot stretch panel that shows the brothers stumbling on some kind of electrical energy in a side alley. Not only has the strategic use of flow from the first to the last panel built an energy in their rhythmic layout, they also intensify our suspense by creating a pause before we know what this is. We have to take the time to physically turn the page to see what it is.

This can work well, too, even when the choice is to use a traditional nine-panel grid format. In *Blue Beetle, Vol. 1: Metamorphosis* (2012) Ig Guara uses the visuals to give dramatic shape to Jaime Reyes's transformation:

Figure 67. Jaime Reyes transforms into the Blue Bettle in *Blue Beetle, Vol. 1: Metamorphosis* (2012).

As we move down the page and from one tier of panels to the next, we experience certain inbuilt pauses (our eyes shift direction). Guara perfectly coordinates this with larger shifts in camera lens focus. Our perceptual, emotional, and interpretive systems have time to make the increased shifts as we move more and more toward a close-up of Reyes's pain. That is, while Guara chooses to repeat from one tier to the next the same sized and shaped panels (three per tier and four tiers all together), the rhythm works well to build us toward the final close-up panel; the panels don't take away from the energy of the shift in lens. Rather, they help cue us to be ready for a dramatic change in the story. (The use of symmetry where, for instance, a first panel mirrors the last panel on a page layout can intensify our meaning making concerning themes of duality.)

The energy of the page comes from the choice of "lens," with the layout taking a back seat. If the page had both movements (shift in panel size and layout along with lens changes), it would likely over-determine the action. We might simply shut off and not experience vicariously Reyes's pain. We turn the page (a physical disruption in the story flow itself) and, *bam*, we have a full page (worm's-eye-view to make him seem even more powerful) of Reyes transformed into an angry (monstrous-looking), mightily powerful Blue Beetle.

Figure 68. Ig Guara's splash page of Reyes's transformation in *Blue Beetle, Vol. 1: Metamorphosis* (2012).

Ig Guara's deft skill with the visual device of panel layout and angle not only build toward this moment of transformation, but ask that we go back and see how it is that he created such motion, rhythmic dynamism, and kinetic force. (For more on the layout, see Madden and Abel, *Mastering Comics*.) In many ways, then, the layout is a foundational shaping device in comic book storytelling. This is where the artist can infuse the story with the dynamism created by movement between and within panels.

Comic book artists can and do (as artists in the visual arts have done) exercise a conservative or a radically exploratory approach to perspective. Just as Picasso dashed to the side perspective and its laws with Cubism, we see with Joe Quesada's art for *Daredevil: Parts of a Hole* the choice to defy perspectival conventions of superhero comics in his geometrizing of Echo's coming of age (see Figure 30).

Quesada chooses to visualize objects and people from a multiplicity of perspectives; he uses his artful hand to show an object from an *impossible* simultaneity of direction. This requires the artist's distilling relationships of space and form all around us, then re-creating in the art of the panel.

Artists like Guara and Quesada want to breathe life into the geometric shapes used—they want their visuals to fill the stories with the action and movement of life. Because comic books operate so foundationally on their visual shaping devices, we don't want to read a superhero comic book where there is no movement, action; even if a dialogue is dynamic, if we only see panel after panel of heads talking to one another, it's boring. There needs to be a creation of movement, of action—*doing*.

I already mentioned how shifts in perspective can create movement in a comic. These are the many angles available to show characters performing—*acting*. Joe Quesada's choice to shift angles when portraying Echo (*Daredevil: Parts of a Hole*) is his way of dynamically framing her character (her body) literally in action. We see this when he visually portrays her dancing.

Quesada's choice of angles makes the difference between a static series of panels, where all the characters appear to be the same size and framed from the same direction, and those panels where characters are drawn from different angles. He has us looking up at the scene, and down at the scene, altering also our meaning making of Echo.

Figure 69. Echo's education of the senses through dance in *Daredevil: Parts of a Hole* (2010).

Of course, there are so many other subtle visual devices that artists use all the time to create action and movement in otherwise static images (panels), including, of course, the technique of foreshortening. On the cover of the New 52's *Justice League of America*

#2 (May 2013) the artists use this technique to present a kinetic (pissed-off and angry) Green Lantern.

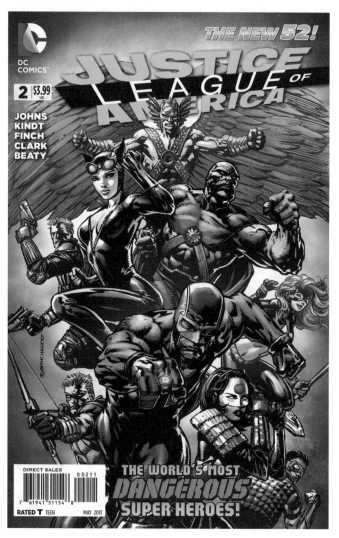

Figure 70. Cover of *Justice League of America* #2 (May 2013).

The action comes out at us, and with it the emotions of the characters. The visuals here are so effective that the phrase that appears at the bottom of the cover page—"The World's Most *Dangerous* Super Heroes!"—is not only unnecessary, it also overdetermines the image. And, of course, artists can decide to use the device of foreshortening within the comic book.

○○○

Of course, a lot more can be said about visual shaping devices, including how at a very basic level they work to give a visual representation of the Latinx superheroes that are the focus of this book. To different degrees, the artist integrates the ethnicity or Latinoness in his or her character. This includes brown coloring, hairstyle, clothing, and any other ethnic visual descriptor.

As I pointed out in the first chapter of this book, many of the earlier Latino superhero characters looked more white European (criollo) than mestizo in complexion and facial bone structure. However, there are those artists like Joe Quesada who have drawn Latino superheroes who are not only dark but who actively identify as Blatino and with a Caribbean heritage. I already mentioned in chapter 1 his visual rendering of Ogun as dark-complexioned with cornrow-braided hair. He's a visual snapshot of a Blatinidad, both Latino and black Caribbean in biological and cultural origin. And I also mentioned how Sara Pichelli's art and coloring breathes a dynamism into the Blatino Miles Morales.

Additionally, I mentioned how Mark Brooks's visual shaping of Anya Corazon as Araña infuses her with more readily identifiable Latina features that are somewhat lost when she grows up to become Spider-Girl. When she becomes Spider-Girl, artists Clayton Henry and Sergio Cariello decide to cover most of her body in a spandex outfit. In the young Anya, we see details of her face and her strong stance; we also see an urban, mixed-race high school.

I end this discussion on the geometrizing of story in superhero comics that feature Latinos with the reminder that, while I consider visual elements to be more dominant in the shaping of plot and character, the experience of reading/viewing comics involves our attending to both the visual *and* the verbal elements. And, while the visuals give shape to the story, they also supply important storyworld elements, such as what a character looks like and how he or she feels and moves (*acts*) in the world. And the verbal ingredients can and do give shape to plot and character elements.

Figure 71. Miles Morales fights Venom in *Ultimate Comics Spider-Man*, vol. 2, #22 (April 2013).

When identifying visual devices like the line as the mark of the author/creator and also as *the* foundation of comics, for instance, we have to be careful not to separate form from content. To understand the way that DC and Marvel create comics with Latinx superheroes we must consider comics as a *storytelling system* that unifies the visual and verbal storytelling arts. Comics tell stories in their unification of form (the toolbox of geometric devices) and textual/verbal content (characterization, plot, and theme). As I've already touched on in the earlier sections of this book, when one or the other comes up short, the comic book falls flat. That is, when there is a lack of the use of formal visual shaping devices, the story falls flat; also, when there is a lack of content shaping devices, the

Figure 72. Brook's Anya Corazon as Araña in *Araña, Vol. 1: Heart of the Spider.*

Figure 73. Henry and Cariello's spandexed Anya as Spider-Girl in *Spider-Girl* #8 (2010).

story falls flat. When either or both fail to make new and innovate our sense of a Latinx superhero character and story, it literally becomes a chore to move from one page and even one panel to the next to get to the story. Both the visuals and the verbal elements inseparably give shape to the comic book. As Thomas Wartenberg remarks, "Comics give images and text equal ontological priority in determining the story-world the comic creates and in providing reader-viewers with the enjoyment they get from the comic" (101).

Storyfying the Geometry

Clearly, the *geometrizing* of the story is important in DC and Marvel comics. However, the experience of reading comics is a visual and verbal gestaltic whole. We travel back and forth seamlessly between visual and written elements. We carefully look over the visuals and admire the art *as well as* follow and assimilate the textual elements: narrative voice, dialogue, thoughts, and the like. We view *and* read comics precisely because of the interplay of the visual with the verbal elements as they give shape to the story.

These foundational story elements are crucial to completing and intensifying the visuals. They *storyfy* the geometry, so to speak. The first page of *Batman: Knightfall*, vol. 1, includes a narrator. Here, the team of writers (Chuck Dixon, Alan Grant, and Doug Moench) decides to include just enough textual description to enrich our experience of the visual. The comic opens with the narrator announcing, "Emboldened by the goings-on in nearby Cuba, the people rose up" (8). Then the narrator continues, "But the ruling Junta here was not so lazy or so blind as the masters of Cuba" (8).

These two sentences, which appear in the two separate jagged-lined boxes positioned at the left top of the first panel of the comic, work with the visuals to efficiently locate the reader in the time and space of the story. We are in the slaughter of war (bloodied bodies lying on the ground) vaguely around the time of the Cuban revolution and in a tropical place (palm trees). The verbal and visual ingredients work together to create a gestalt of time/space—something that would be less efficiently done if only the visuals or only the verbal shaping devices were used.

The strategic choice of a few words is all it takes to situate, then launch, the story. Had there been more of a verbal presence, it might have tipped more into the world of illustrated book than comic. And had there been a lack of verbal ingredient, more panels would have been necessary to locate us in specifics of time and space. We would need more visuals to guide our gap-filling mechanisms so as not to wander too far afield from the story. As we move down this first page of *Knightfall*, the visuals are dominant but work within a seamless and careful interplay with the verbal

Toward a Theory of LatinX Comic Book Superheroes

Figure 74. The text anchors readers in the time and place of the storyworld in *Batman: Knightfall*, vol. 1 (2012).

elements that allow for the complex layering of narratives that dynamically move the story forward.

In this chapter I focus on the narrative devices (verbal, theme, plot, and so on) used to give shape to Latinos in DC and Marvel comics. From the writer composing the script to the actual devices used, such as text in boxes (narrator and character) and words in balloons, among others, we see how the *storyfying* of geometry is a necessary part of the creation of comic book storytelling.

The comic often begins with a script. This requires a great will to style on the part of the writer: a great facility with language, a sharp yet abundant imagination, and a responsibility to the subject matter. When the writer (or writing team, as is often the case with DC and Marvel) sets pen to paper to write the script, he or she already has centrally in mind that the words will work in conjunction with images. The writer selects certain details that will variously guide, intensify, and reverberate with the visuals. Because of the presence of the visual shaping devices, the writers are free to use their words to describe—or not—a character or setting.

In superhero comics, what is of paramount importance when it comes to storyfying the geometry is the strategic use of the verbal devices to *move* the story along in ways whereby the progression of visuals (panels) is not static. As the story propels forward, it acquires a thickness because of the interplay of the verbal with the visual elements that give shape to characters, themes, and plots.

In mainstream superhero comics, I see three main ways that writers use verbal shaping devices to storyfy the geometry:

1. The writer(s) conceives of the written story in terms of its geometry: the visual layout, drawing of character and mise-en-scene, and so on.
2. The writer(s) roughs out how the visual shaping devices are to be used. That is, the writer creates a storyboard of sorts that includes lots of detail about the page layout, perspective, movement, and angle as well as objects and their placement within the panel.
3. The writer(s) creates this basic script, which is then given to the penciler, inker, and colorist, who then distill and reconstruct the story with the use of visual shaping devices.

From the moment we first encounter the comic book on the bookstore shelf to the opening of the first page, the verbal shaping devices are present. Some comics have more than just the title and other information on the cover page. They also might include descriptors. For instance, David Finch (artist) provides a dynamic visual of Cisco as Vibe on the cover of *Vibe* #1 (February 2013). With great energy, Finch geometrizes his transmitting of an electrokinetic force field from his fisted hands. And there also appears the phrase: "The Unlikeliest Hero!"

Finch's geometric shapes convey much energy and semantic meaning, but it's the text that provides nuance. We know from the visuals that he's powerful: his vibrational powers are breaking up the earth. But we could never know from the visuals alone that he's "the unlikeliest hero." The text efficiently adds nuance to

Figure 75. David Finch's cover for *Justice League of America's Vibe* #1 (February 2013).

the geometric shaping devices. And once we're in the storyworld proper, this becomes even more apparent. For instance, how would one visually portray the following information Agent Gunn gives to Cisco: "You just wielded vibrational powers you acquired from exposure to the interdimensional forces that hold the myriad alternate realities together . . . to stop a third grader with a sweet tooth. Bit of overkill, wouldn't you say?" (*New 52 Justice League of American's Vibe* #2, May 2013). Generally speaking, the greater the presence of words, the more reading time and, therefore, the slower the story moves forward in its pure geometrizing effect. And the more words, the less co-creating takes place; the accumulation of concepts, thoughts, and feelings conveyed by the text put certain constraints on our decoding and reimagining process. The net effect: too much text slows down the action *and* diminishes the degree of co-creative reader involvement.

At the most basic level of meaning making, a given comic's verbal design *names* the characters and their superhero alter egos. From Anya Corazon to Maya Lopez to Cisco Ramon to Hector Ayala and Angela del Torro to Renee María Montoya—the names identify them as *Latino*. Whether or not the visuals give the *color* (shades of brown), the names can and do identify the superhero as Latinx.

Also important, names can be used to create tensions between a given superhero's identities. There's visible brown Miles Morales as public civilian. And there's Miles Morales as masked and costumed (nonethnic) Spider-Man. Bendis creates a certain tension in the comic based on a duality constructed by the interplay of the visuals (phenotype) with the textual (name): Brown (Morales) vs. non-ethnic (Spidey). We see the same for most Latino superheroes who *mask* their Latinidad, playing to the convention in superhero comics of opening up the character for greater reader identification. As Stan Lee sums up, "Nearly *every* reader could imagine himself beneath that mask—age, and background and ethnicity didn't matter" (96).

As a given comic book story unfolds, the verbal ingredients continue to enrich and nuance characterization, intensifying our engagement. For instance, the identification of the loss of a parent or parents through verbal textual means allows creators to infuse emotional depth and cognitive complexity into a Latino superhero. Those like Maya Lopez and Bane are orphans. Others like Miles Morales and Vibe have lost one parent: both Cisco (Vibe) and Miles (Spider-Man) lost mothers and live with single dads. With many readers having been raised by one parent, there's much to relate to. But there's also something that speaks to the Latino experience— that somehow our demographic group has been orphaned within the Unites States' socioeconomic system. This adds to the equally relatable dimension of Latino superheroes being self-constructed—built through physical and mental work, and not superheroic as a matter of birth.

This Latinidad can be further enhanced (and playfully so) within the verbal design of the dialogue. Bilingual play to identify generational contact with Latinoness: In *Blue Beetle, Vol. 1: Metamorphosis*, writer Tony Bedard chooses to give Jaime Reyes and his family members a bilingual identity. They move seamlessly between English and Spanish. In the kitchen the mother tells Jaime, for instance: "Lo siento, mijo, pero there's no way I'm letting you go to la casa Ampara Cardenas!*" Bedard includes a playful wink, especially for Latino readers. The inclusion of an asterisk guides us to a text box in the bottom right corner of the panel that reads: "*Translated from the Spanglish." And, as is typical of Latinos at home, Jaime responds in Spanish, "Pero Mami, ¿por qué? Did Brenda's tía do something to you?" Being responsible to his subject matter, Bedard's done his homework concerning the different uses of language within the Latino community. Not all Latinos are bilingual. To capture this (and *naturalize* it as also normal) Bedard creates Jaime's best friend, Paco, as a dominant English speaker, who only occasionally punctuates his sentences with Spanish slang, like "No manches, wey!" Important, too, is the realistic way in which Bedard does all this moving back and forth between languages. That is, he captures the rhythms and cadences of Latino speakers in ways that clearly show that he's making an attempt to re-create the way Latinos move between English and Spanish in everyday interactions. While the phonetic spellings don't always get it right ("wey" should be "guey," for instance), unlike earlier periods in the history of representing Latinos in comic books, Bedard is trying to capture a real-sounding dialogue (how Latinos speak) to reconstruct fictional Latinos who give verbal energy to the story and who will likely engage more real Latino readers.

The verbal shaping of the story includes, also, the presence of a narrator. Sometimes this appears in the form of an omniscient third-person voice or as a voice we identify with a character but that speaks above and outside the events of the storyworld. It is the narrator's voice that functions as the constant guiding presence in the opening chapters of *Knightfall*. It provides the reader with that sense of depth of Bane's interiority as we follow his education of the senses from child to man, from weak to strong in body and mind. On one occasion, the narrator informs us: "There was power in knowing things. When he had consumed all of the prison library, he sought more" (27). While the visuals provide the big brushstrokes of how he grows and transforms from child to man, it is the narrator's commentary that provides the nuances of detail in how he has educated his mind and body through physical exercise, meditation, and studious dedication to reading important philosophical and literary works.

The verbal elements allow the creator(s) to provide insight into any given character. They allow the creator to invest a character with nuanced thoughts and feelings. The verbal elements provide the reader with a compass direction for more nuanced evaluation of character than might be present if only the visual shaping devices were used. And, while earlier re-creations of Latinos in comics tended to slip into a lazy use of the verbal elements (Vibe's truncated, nonsensical English phrases, for instance), today we're seeing a greater willfulness that intensifies not only our engagement with the Latino character but also our interest in the comic book taken as a whole. *Spider-Girl*, vol. 2, #5 (May 2011) is a case in point. Here author Paul Tobin uses a variety of traditional narrative devices, such as third-person narration, first-person monologue, and dialogue between characters. But he also uses Twitter as a way to give nuance to character *and* to add energy to the kinetic geometric shaping of the narrative by artists Matthew Southworth with Sergio Cariello and colorists Chris Sotomayor and Edgar Delgado.

For Latina Anya Corazon as the older teen Spider-Girl, tweeting becomes a kind of public ongoing diary for her fans. It also provides Tobin an additional verbal device for immersing us readers into her interior states of mind, revealing to us her anxieties and insecurities. On another occasion, she tweets, "I wonder if I sound Tough. Does Captain America ever worry about his Voice Cracking?" Tobin chooses to use this verbal shaping device to make *public* Spider-Girl's private reflections on her contemporary world (social, natural, and physical), and the expression of anxieties very much reflects those of teens who inhabit social margins: young women of color. That is, in *Spider-Girl* the geometrizing of the story, along with its textual shaping devices, allows Tobin et al. to create a complex thinking and feeling Latina superhero.

Figure 76. Latina Spider-Girl texting in *Spider-Girl*, vol. 2, #5 (May 2011).

○○○

The visuals and coloring can and do identify characters as Latinx. The verbal elements add depth and complexity to characters *as* Latinx. However, it is not always the case that both visual and verbal elements work together to create a strong sense of Latinidad—and this even in today's comics. For instance, while the name "Anya Corazon" and the written backstory identify Spider-Girl as Latina, the visuals describe her as light-skinned and with Anglo features. Certainly with our histories of being colonized, we are mestizo, with some of us having lighter skin and more European features. However, we are also born with dark skin and more indigenous features. No matter the degree of presence of a willfulness to reconstruct Latinoness through verbal means (narrative backstory, dialogue, and paratextual websites), since the first appearance of Latinos with characters like The Whip and later El Gaucho, DC and Marvel tend to create lighter-skinned, Caucasian-featured Latinx superheroes.

There are, of course, important exceptions. In the first chapter of this book I mentioned several exceptions within the DC and Marvel universe. They include, for instance, George Pérez's White Tiger; Marv Wolfman and Jerry Ordway's Gangbuster; Chris Claremont and Bob McLeod's Sunspot; Will Pfeifer and Patrick Gleason's Aquagirl; Felipe Smith and Tradd Moore's new Ghost Rider; Miles Morales as the Blatino-identified Spidey; Keith Giffen, John Rogers, and Cully Hamner's new Blue Beetle; and Joe Quesada's Afrolatino Santerian superhero team. When the artists choose to create phenotypically dark and/or non-Caucasian featured Latinx superheroes, they offer not only a richer and more complete representation of what it means to look and be Latinx but another way for the writers to efficiently use the verbal elements to further complicate Latinx identity and experience by offering a greater range of backstories.

As I wrap up this discussion of the importance of the willful use of the verbal elements in the shaping of Latino superheroes—and the importance of this along with the visual devices—I would like to mention how they give robust shape to dominant themes and plots woven in and around Latinx characters: vigilantism and the bildungsroman. In the mainstream comic book universe, the verbal elements tend to be used to plot Latinx characters who work hard to become superheroes and who seek revenge against a deeply corrupt society. I mentioned already Chuck Dixon, Graham Nolan, and Doug Moench's creation of the Latino supervillain Bane as well as Rob Williams and Matthew Clark's Alejandra as Ghost Rider. I mentioned also the different incarnations of El Diablo: Gerard Jones and Mike Parobeck's Rafael Sandoval as El Diablo, and Jai Nitz, Phil Hester, and Ande Parks's Chato Santana. These are but a few of the many instances where verbal elements give shape to backstories and information about their respective education and journeys to becoming who they are. In the case of El Diablo, this ultimately ends up tied to his vigilantism: his need to take justice into his own hands and with the blessing of the community.

The verbal elements in mainstream comics, then, have helped create Latinos as self-made superheroes who tend to take justice into their own hands to help the community. These superheroes tend, also, to work within collectives—whether with the blessing of the community or alongside other superheroes like the Suicide Squad or X-Men. This is to say, the verbal elements allow the creators to make Latinos who arguably might appeal more to Latino readers who share similar histories and experiences; who have not been born with superpowers, silver spoons, or privilege, but have had to build themselves into superheroes who largely give back; and who mostly fight for the community (and within communities). Good writing along with dynamic visuals can convey Latino superheroes who build their intelligence and strength through experience and work, and not as genetically preordained beings. In this way, the willful *geometrizing* of the story and *storyfying* of the geometry can and do work together to make compelling Latinx superheroes.

Chapter 3

MULTIMEDIATED LATINX SUPERHEROES

Animated Super-Lats

Before launching into a discussion of Latinx superheroes in animation (followed by TV shows, then film), let me briefly remind you of
a shared history of growth and cross-pollination among the comic
book, cartoon, TV, and film storytelling formats. In *Projections*,
Jared Gardner does a masterful job explaining the coevolution of
film and comics. We can add to this TV, film, and video games—
given that there are few Latino superheroes who have crossed over
into video games—but I'll leave that discussion for another time
and place. (Latino scholars such as Osvaldo Cleger, Phillip Penix-
Tadson, and myself have written on Latinos and video games, but
more globally.) Indeed, an exploration of Latino superheroes in
animation, TV, and film demonstrates the differing degrees of willful presence in giving shape to such storyworlds.

In-print superhero comics tend to provide the origin stories
or protoworlds for re-creations in the animation, film, and TV formats. However, given that these are all narrative media that have
come into their own during the twentieth century, we also see a
cross-pollination of shaping devices between them. Today more
than ever we see this intermixing both subtly and explicitly in the
way that framing, editing, perspectival angles, and actual drawing inform the shaping of comic book, animation, film, and TV
storyworlds. And, with superhero comic book storyworlds, we
see the movement of the same characters (and often plots) across
the different media. This happens in obvious and subtle ways. For
instance, many film stars today are looking like Chris Evans with
huge muscled bodies, chiseled jaw lines, and expressionistic acting.
They appear in non-superhero films, but do so with bodybuilder
looks and exaggerated comic book emotion effects. And, there
are directors like Christopher Nolan who pushed away from the
use of the canted shot and dizzying amount of lens shift edits à la

Schumacher's *Batman & Robin* (1997) to more subtly bring a comic book aesthetic into his Dark Knight trilogy with the use of IMAX lensing and Hans Zimmer's epic heroic music scores. Bryan Singer also brings the comic book effect into his *X-Men* series by creating kinetic shots that shift perspective on a single figure or object in ways that crisscross perspective planes. And, with advances in CGI we see not only the making of comic book films in subtle ways but also the potential for different animated storyworld creations.

One way or another, scholars have begun to excavate exactly what happens in these cross-pollinations and passages from one medium to another. For instance, in her foundational book, *Theory of Adaptation*, Linda Hutcheon understood this movement of character and story as well as the intertwining of shaping devices as triggering a certain pleasure in audiences as they encountered a narrative that was at once recognizable *and* modified. And, Brian McHale talks of these transfers and transformations as "versions" of the protoworld in "a later text that repeats it in some way and to some greater or lesser degree, short of point-for-point duplication." For McHale, there are versions that "remake" the original with a maximum of correspondence, those that "remediate" as a "more or less *faithful* transposition of the original into a different medium," and then those that "rewrite" and have a "substantial correspondence with their originals, but also substantial deviations." In "Transmedial Storytelling and Transfictionality," Marie-Laure Ryan offers similarly generative concepts for understanding the re-creative moves between protoworld and secondary storyworlds. For Ryan, the concept of "expansion" identifies how the re-created secondary storyworld enhances our understanding of the protoworld by introducing new elements into the fiction; "modification" identifies changes to the protoworld and creates a different trajectory to character and plot; and "transposition" identifies how the secondary cultural artifact has carried the protoworld into different time/spaces but without changing the protoworld's fundamental blueprint of plot, character, and the like (paraphrase 365).

The superhero comic book universe is rife with infinite variations on these "versions," "expansions," "modifications," and "transpositions." We know from the biographies of Latino creators of comics that they metabolize and make new versions from all these different narrative formats. Those like Gus Arriola, Frank

Espinosa, Rafael Rosado, Octavio Rodriguez, and David Marquez, among many others, first cut their teeth as visual-verbal storytellers working in the world of animation. These and other Latino comic book creators had cartoons, TV shows, and films as part of their education in the visual-verbal arts. For instance, Carlos Saldaña, creator of *Burrito*, speaks about being hugely influenced by Disney cartoons and Japanese manga as he developed his unique comic book style (see *Your Brain on Latino Comics*). The Latino creator of *Sonambulo*, Rafael Navarro, reflects on his own education as one filled to the brim with "Fellini, Leone, Orson Welles, Fritz Lang, Howard Hawks, Akira Kurosawa, Federico Curiel, David Lean, David Lynch, Robert Rodriguez, and Ed Wood." In each he learned how to lay out his panels like a film with "the establishing shot, cut to a medium shot, then pull back, then cut to a close-up, all for dramatic purposes" (*Your Brain on Latino Comics*, 227). And, like many of the Latino comic book pioneers, Fernando Rodriguez (*Aztec of the City*) grew up with black-and-white TV shows, such as *Time Tunnel*, *Land of the Giants*, and *Twilight Zone*, as well as cartoons like *Fantastic Four*, *Sub-Mariner*, *Captain America*, *The Herculoids*, *Speed Racer*, *Space Ghost*, *Batman*, *Green Lantern*, *Shazam*, *Wonder Woman*, and *Baretta* (*Your Brain on Latino Comics*). This is to say that I'm not making a huge leap when moving from comic books to animation to TV to film in this exploration of the construction of Latinx superheroes in the mainstream.

And this makes sense in a film, TV, and animation marketplace where superhero storyworlds seem to be generating huge profits. In 2000, Bryan Singer's *X-Men* opened to a $54 million weekend. As Liam Burke remarks, it "ushered in an era of unprecedented comic book adaptation production by Hollywood studios" (5). Today, a film like *Suicide Squad* can bring in more than $746 million. With season 4 of *Agents of S.H.I.E.L.D.*, ABC's viewership rose to 5.549 million. Of course, more money doesn't always mean increased presence of Latinos. While some prime-time TV comic book shows appear to finally be realizing that in their reconstructed expansions, modifications, and transpositions there are protoworld Latino superheroes to draw from, we still continue to see a general trend to exclude more than include.

o o o

As I've discussed, creators of Latinos in mainstream comics *geometrize* the story and *storyfy* the geometry. And, as I've shown, some creative teams do this with a greater visual and verbal willfulness than others; some do so with greater writing and visual storytelling skills than others; and some evince a greater responsibility to Latinx history, culture, and language. And, while today we see an uptick in quantity and quality of Latinos appearing in the DC and Marvel universes, they continue to remain vastly underrepresented. Latinx superheroes (and supervillains) are but a sprinkle (and sometimes only spicy) within a supra-galaxy filled with A-lister Anglo superheroes. The picture doesn't improve much when I shift focus to Latinx superheroes in other mainstream media, such as animation (cartoons), TV shows, and film. In fact, it gets worse. In this third chapter, I explore how in the re-creation of "versions" of comic book storyworlds—specifically in animation, TV shows, and film—there's often a modification that simplifies or that completely erases Latinos/as.

Many of us grew up with superhero comic books—and superhero cartoons on Saturday morning TV. Some of us even recall the occasional spotting of a Latino during those gluttonous Saturday morning cartoon feasts. One such Latino, El Dorado, appeared in *The Super Friends* (1981)—a cartoon based on DC's Justice League of America. Eager for any kind of non-Anglo superhero to appear in cartoons and more than wet behind the ears, we likely missed the utter *lack* of a will to style in his creation. ABC's creative team certainly didn't care about getting El Dorado's history and cultural references correct. He's a hodgepodge: named after the myth of the city of gold in Peru, *yet* his gold-laden, hieroglyphed, wide-collar neck and chest piece features the Mexican symbol of the eagle. Is he Mexican? Is he Peruvian? His exotic, sexualized look, his thick accented and truncated English ("E-L D-O-R-A-D-O, A-m-i-g-o," "o-n-e t-r-i-c-k-y h-o-m-b-r-e"), and his preternatural knowledge of pre-Columbian culture serve *only* to help rescue his fellow Anglo Super Friends. In other words, ABC's animation team decided to go more for the hodgepodge noble savage who cleans up messes for the Anglo Super Friends than to create an engaging Latinx superhero.

While we might have been forgiving of ABC's creation of El Dorado because he was the lone Latino in cartoons, it's clear today that from an aesthetic and cultural point of view he was a bust. There's a diminished will to style present here, one that simplifies and essentializes in a careless and lazy manner. The creators didn't do a modicum of research concerning pre-Columbian artifacts and history.

Today we see the creation of a greater variety of Latino superheroes in cartoons. And in their making there's less of a will to throw all cultural references into the pot and stir. Indeed, we're seeing the re-creation of DC and Marvel Latino superheroes like Tejano Jaime Reyes (Blue Beetle), Afrolatino Miles Morales (Spider-Man), and Sam Alexander as the new Nova. We're also witnessing the re-creation of a few Latina superheroes, like the hybrid feline-Latina Rosabelle Mendez as Pantha, the pyroplasmic Latina Beatriz Bonilla da Costa as Green Fury (Green Flame or Fire), and Nuyorican Ava Ayala as White Tiger. In mainstream cartoons we also have the creation of animated originals like the speedy Guatemalan émigré twins, Mas Y Menos, who appear in *Teen Titans*. And we have a few nonmainstream superhero creations, such as Adam de le Peña's El Jefe in *Minoriteam* and Jorge Gutierrez's eponymous El Tigre.

Of course, as with any and all cultural phenomena, both form and content matter. In the case of cartooned Latinx superheroes, it matters if the characters are skillfully animated *and* anchored in a coherent *and* recognizable Latinoness—and this even if the characters are tied to the ready-packaged backstories of their in-print comic book original identities. For them to *pop* and engage us in their new cartoon shape, the artists (illustrators, camera operators, and computer programmers), screenwriters, music scorers, and voice-over actors (Latinos, and not Anglos) must fully realize them within this drawn *motion* storytelling format. That is, there must be a willful distillation and re-creation at the level of the art, writing, and voice-over acting that give new life even to those Latino superheroes whom we already know from other superhero comic book storytelling formats.

Mainstream cartoons that feature Latinx superheroes mostly follow a, say, realist approach to their storytelling. When White Tiger leaps, she does so in a storyworld constructed to resemble our world, that's governed by gravity, for instance; and even if her movements are gravity defying, we recognize them as being like our movements. This is to say, mainstream cartoons that feature Latinx superheroes follow the kind of realism (a mimetic and realist impulse) seen with Disney cartoons. In *Animation: Genre and Authorship*, Paul Wells sums up the Disney effect as a "hyper-realist styling" that is "informed by close engagement with authentic, anatomically viable movement forms" (4). Wells further comments, "This drive for 'hyper-realism' in Disney films seemed to fundamentally refute the intrinsic vocabulary of the form—that is, the ability to challenge the parameters of live-action illusionism, and the very tenets of 'realism' that this predominantly embraces" (9). Like Disney cartoons, mainstream animations that feature Latinx superheroes today use the techniques of time, sound, color, and multiplane perspective at the service of creating this *reality effect*, but do so in ways that play it safe. That is, they seek to create cartoons that adhere to natural laws (gravity and biology, for instance) to present in a reality-based, logical way their defiance. Blue Beetle defies gravity—a gravity present for all those non-superhero characters that have a tellurian hold on him when he's not propelled by his scarab-activated high-tech body suit; he's under the same tellurian hold as all other human characters. And, when Ayala as White Tiger defends the innocent, and animation writers and designers build a recognizable storyworld filled with the recognizable everyday conventions of social behavior actions: those who harm innocents are *bad* and those who protect innocents are good.

The "versions" of Latino superheroes that appear in the cartoon-world landscape tend to operate in fairly conventional ways. They tend not to make new in their various expansions, modifications, and transpositions. Even though animation could present new ways of experiencing the Latino superhero characters and plots, animation studios tend to play it safe.

There are several animated versions made from the DC universe that think to include Latino superheroes. Director Peter Rida Michail and writer John Loy's "Más y Menos" episode in *Teen Titans Go!* (season 1, episode 48, April 2014) re-create DC's Spanish-only speaking Latino (Guatemalan) superhero twins as more shapely and round children; in Geoff John's in-print comic, *Teen Titans*, vol. 3, #38 (2006), they appear as muscled young men.

The animation team chose to further shape the Latino super twins' Latino identity by casting Freddy Rodriguez as their voice.

Figure 77. Más y Menos in Cartoon Network's *Teen Titans Go!* (episode 48, April 2014).

Moreover, in an animation aimed at a young viewership we have the choice to re-create two Latinx superhero children in a positive light: their superspeed travel generates when they touch one another; their action is familial and collective. And, the show doesn't capitulate to English-only viewers. Only when Más y Menos speak to the other characters do subtitles appear in English for the viewer, revealing how the English-speaking characters often misunderstand the twins. In contrast to many mainstream shows generally, here's a superhero show aimed at young audiences where the writing guides them to laugh at the non-Spanish-speaking characters, and not the Spanish-speaking Latinos. Michail and Loy re-create Más y Menos as children and for a young audience in ways that defy the stereotypes of Latinos. Arguably, in their animated version of Geoff John's in-print protoworld the creators could have created more compelling Latino twin superheroes. With the creation of a backstory—that they are the Maya twins Hunahpu and Xbalanque depicted in the Popol Vuh—this important history could have added richness to the story and our engagement with it.

And, we see in James Tucker's and Michael Jelenic's *Batman: The Brave and the Bold* (*Cartoon Network*, 2008–2011) the inclusion of Latinx superheroes—the green-flamed Beatriz Bonilla da Costa as Fire and Jaime Reyes (voiced variously by Anglos Will Friedle and Jason Marsden) as Blue Beetle, but in ways that modify the in-print protoworld in areas that count: the casting of non-Latino voice actors such as Will Friedle and Jason Marsden to characterize Jaime Reyes as Blue Beetle. When we hear Jaime code-switch Spanish and English, this animated version of the Blue Beetle superhero becomes less convincing—and less worth the audience's emotional investment. And, this creative cartoon team also chooses to modify the in-print protoworld by re-creating Reyes as an impulsive adolescent (and not the thoughtful Latino of the comic) who serves as comic relief and as an irritant to the more staid and even-tempered Batman. We see something similar with director Ben Jones and his animation creative team that choose to use Anglo Diane Delano as the voice of the Latina *luchador* superhero Pantha in *Teen Titans* (episode 63, "Calling All Titans," 2006). Delano lays it on thick with a faux Spanish accent, speaking a truncated, deliberate, staccato-rhythmed English, loading Pantha down with all the stereotypical linguistic markers. And replicating uncritically a divide-and-conquer ideology, the show has Pantha use her superhuman strength and "Claw" to smack down a super-villain, but it's a Mexican supervillain.

There are creative teams that put more thought into their Latinx superhero animated modifications. I think of director Melchior Zwyer and writer Kevin Hopps, who create a version of Jaime as Blue Beetle in *Young Justice* (2012–) that allows us to more fully imagine him as a Latino. They write him as smart and with agency (and not Latino buffoon, as in *Batman*). They also cast a Latino, Eric Lopez, as the voice actor. That is, this creative team's re-created drawing-in-motion version of Blue Beetle invites our co-participation.

Figure 78. Jaime Reyes discovers the scarab in *Young Justice Invasion*, "Before the Dawn."

In *Justice League Unlimited* (2004–2006), the Portuguese American director Joaquim Dos Santos and his creative team are also careful to cast Latino/a voices to give shape to their two characters, Hawkgirl (voiced by María Canals Barrera) and El Diablo (voiced by Nestor Carbonell). These directors seem especially attuned to how the choice of voice actor functions as an important shaping device in the re-creation of Latinx superheroes and in the way audience invests in and engages with these characters. This is to say, animated versions of in-print comic book storyworlds that choose to re-create Latinx superheroes can work or not depending on modifications such as choice of voice actor. If the creators aren't exercising their responsibility to their re-created version of the in-print Latino superhero along with a strong sense of how Latinos speak and act in their everyday life (the building blocks of reality) then the animation rings flat.

Thus far I've focused on animated versions of DC in-print comics. We see a similar pattern with animated versions of Marvel comics, too. In director Tim Maltby and writers Kevin Burke and Chris Wyatt's episode "The Spider-Verse, Part 3" (September 20, 2014) of *Ultimate Spider-Man*, they draw him with tight curled hair and choose to cast African American actor Danny Glover as Miles Morales. That is, they racialize Miles, but in ways that erase his Latino identity. And, when the creative team introduces Ava Ayala in the *Ultimate Spider-Man* episode "Kraven the Hunter" (February 3, 2013), they color her a shade of brown as well as draw her with some non-Caucasian features (wider nose, for instance) and with straight hair to suggest her Puerto Rican Hispanic Caribbean heritage, but they cast an Anglo as her voice actor (Caitlin Taylor Love).

In 2007, Stan Lee and Marv Wolfman decided to create an animation (direct-to-DVD), *The Condor*, that falls outside the Marvel universe and that stands entirely on its own. While *The Condor* received little attention (and the little it did was not favorable), it is the first such animated feature-length narrative to focus on a Latino superhero, Tony Valdez as The Condor. Importantly, Lee and Wolfman make some excellent creative decisions regarding the Latinoness that is shaped by the animation. They chose to cast Wilmer Valderrama as the voice actor who gives auditory shape to Tony Valdez, a Latino skateboard champ who, after his parents are murdered and he's left paralyzed, becomes a nanotech-enabled

Figure 79. Miles Morales as Spider-Man in *Ultimate Spider-Man* (2012–).

Figure 80. Ava Ayala as White Tiger in *Ultimate Spider-Man* (2012–).

speedster superhero. Lee and Wolfman choose not to cast the supervillain as a person of color. Rather, while there is a Latina supervillain, Valeria as Taipan, the character the audience is meant to feel the least sympathy for is the Anglo evildoer, Nigel Harrington. Disabled and Latino, Valdez works with the Latina tomboy and his eventual love interest, Sammi; his cousin, Reuben; and friends such as the wise Polynesian surfer, Dogg, and African American fellow skateboarder, Z-Man, to save the day. The Latinx characters all move easily between speaking English and Spanish. And, Lee and Wolfman re-create Tony from many of the struggles and experiences of Latinx youth today within the community and family. For instance, his parents tend to speak Spanish, and English with an accent. They write the mother, María (voiced by María Conchita Alonso), as having deep roots in her ancestry; she's the one who passes down to Tony (Antoñio) the "The Condor" necklace that he wears. And they write this new generation of Latinos as demanding respect. The young Latina Sammi is a genius tech engineer who gives Tony's skateboard a high-tech makeover and adapts the nanotechnology developed at Valdez Corp to give Tony his superpowered legs. In the end, too, they are careful not to have Tony slip into an assimilationist mode. Rather, they have him fully embrace his Latinx identity, concluding the story with his asking to be called *El* Condor, and not *The* Condor.

At least in the world of animation, animated versions of DC and Marvel in-print comics that feature Latino superheroes appear as a mixed bag, in content and form. While we see some big representational steps forward with Miles Morales, Ava Ayala, the Guatemalan super twins, and Tony Valdez, we also see some equally big moves that push us backward into yesteryear's stereotypes, especially in the casting of Anglos to give auditory shape to the Latino characters.

There are nonmainstream superhero cartoons that make new our perception, thought, and feeling about Latinos. I think of Adam de le Peña's *Minoriteam* (2005–2006) and Jorge Gutierrez's *El Tigre* (2008), which follow the anything-goes, antimimetic approach seen in the cartoons of Tex Avery. In form and substance Tex Avery's approach to animation differed greatly from Walt Disney's. Where Disney used his technical means to create cartoons aimed at fostering close adherence to social and natural laws, Avery made cartoon worlds that pushed at these social and natural boundaries.

While Disney sought conventions that would give the illusion of a nontransgressive, conventional reality, Avery's storyworlds aimed at the extremely unconventional, infusing his works, in Floriane Place-Verghnes's words, with "a certain poetic and oneiric (of dreams) quality" (5). So, while Disney sought to give his cartoon worlds the smooth and polished veneer of a conventional realism, Avery made cartoon worlds that delighted in flaunting their own unbounded possibilities. In Disney, the bad guys are evil in carefully calculated and limited ways, while the good guys are good according to recognized social rules of behavior, and they remain so for all eternity. In Avery, the bad guys are unrestrained rascals, and the good guys are sometimes also dangerously mischievous.

In the flash animation, Tex Avery anything-goes style of *Minoriteam* and *El Tigre* we see other, non-Disney realist modes that vitally work to re-create Latinx superheroes in ways that explode both in form and content Latinx superhero *types*. For instance, in the making of *El Tigre* Jorge Gutierrez refuses to adhere to social and natural conventions. His creation of the thirteen-year-old Manny Rivera as El Tigre is rooted in family (papa as La Pantera and abuelo as Puma Loco) and Latino tradition in ways that are aimed at a Latinx ideal audience: the show entertains through its poking fun at itself and providing inside jokes and allusions that only a Latinx audience would get.

Figure 81. El Tigre vs. Son of Sartana in *El Tigre* (2007–2008).

Gutierrez's Latinx superheroes are not a tourist attraction for Anglo viewers. In matters of content and form Gutierrez's superheroes are created for a Latinx audience. (See also Serrato, "Postmodern Guacamole: Lifting the Lid on *El Tigre: The Adventures of Manny River*.") And, Adam de la Peña uses flash animation in the creation of the superhero El Jefe. El Jefe is overweight, has a huge mustache, wears a gigantic a sombrero as his disguise, and uses a Leafblower 3000 (the deadliest in the universe) to fight white supremacists like Racist Frankenstein. El Jefe is identified as a Mexican with one-eighteenth Viking blood. In the writing and animated drawing, Adam de la Peña uses the shaping device of hyperbole to at once inhabit then explode stereotypes of Latinos.

In closing this discussion of Latino superheroes in animated cartoons, I would like to gesture toward how those like *Minoriteam* and *El Tigre* not only evince a greater will to style in terms of content—de la Peña and Gutierrez know well the stereotypes, inhabit them, and deconstruct them from within—as well as form: flash animation (vs. digital or hand-drawn). De la Peña and Gutierrez embrace the stiltedness of flash animation as a way to expose the device, or break the so-called fourth wall. That is, they give exploratory shape to their distillations and re-creations of Latino identities and experiences in ways that at once entertain, affirm, and complicate Latinoness.

Televisualized Caped Crusaders

Before moving into exploring the filmic re-creations or versions (expansions, modifications, and transpositions) of in-print superhero comics, let me discuss a few televisual versions that have made some attempt at creating Latinx superheroes. Mostly, what we see in the televisual versions of in-print comics is a modification process that erases, assimilates (Anglos in brownface), re-racializes as a non-Latino Other (usually as African American), and/or exoticizes Latinos.

Many of today's superhero TV shows seem to forget that Latinos exist both in the superhero comic book universe and as part of the U.S. demographic at large. In network and cable TV we see few Latino superheroes, few Latinos generally. In fact, we're represented in less than 2 percent of TV shows overall. In spite of this consistent move to erase our 18 percent demographic presence from prime time, there have been a few shows that chose to re-create us, and in hyperexaggerated ways. The Latino as hypersexual comic buffoon rears its ugly head in 2001, with Ben Edlund and Barry Sonnenfeld's re-creation for Fox of Edlund's 1986 original comic book, *The Tick*. While they exercise a modicum of willfulness in their casting, Cuban American Nestor Gastón Carbonell plays the role of the goateed Batmanuel, the writing and visualization of Carbonell as this Latino superhero slips into a lazy, pejorative stereotype: he speaks English with a thick Spanish accent and includes with his Batman get-up a gold chain and a shiny codpiece (which doubles as his wallet). He drives a gold Buick with a license plate that reads: "BATLOVE." His superpower: lechery. And while the show is meant to be a comedy, because Edlund and Sonnenfeld choose not to infuse any additional textual layers that might lend to the viewer's consuming of this hypersexualized, bumbling Latino buffoon as satirical or parodic, it simply reproduces and reinforces negative stereotypes. In season 1 of the 2016 reboot of *The Tick*, fortunately, Ben Edlund (writer) and Wally Pfister (director) don't reprise the offensive superhero Batmanuel. But it's business as usual with rest of the casting. Anglo Peter Serafinowicz plays the protagonist, The Tick, with a few Latinos cast as sidekicks (Christian Navarro as Sidekick #1) and villains (Latina Yara Martinez as the face-scarred villain Ms. Lint, along with her Latino henchman, Thug #1, played by Berto Colon).

There have been some televisual versions of Latina superheroes from DC's in-print protoworlds, but they are usually hypersexualized. Alfred Gough and Miles Millar's popular, long-running series, *Smallville* (2001–2011), is a case in point. It did make a few attempts at "browning" some of its otherwise all-Anglo superhero landscape by variously introducing *two* Latinx superheroes: Andrea Rojas and Jaime Reyes. In season 5, episode 13, for instance, Gough and Millar re-create a modified version of the in-print Latina superhero Ácrata: "Angel of Vengeance." They still identify her as Andrea Rojas, but they modify her Spanish moniker "Ácrata" (anarchist) with the English "Angel of Vengeance." In the televisual storyworld modification, "Ácrata" is mentioned, but as the name of the organization that her mother worked for before being killed by Luther's father. The televisual Angel of Vengeance appears out of nowhere to save the teen Clark Kent's mother, Martha, from a mugging in the barrio of Metropolis known as Suicide Slum. And there's a further modification. Gough and Millar's Angel of Vengeance is a monolingual English-speaking Latina, in contrast with the protean Ácrata as a monolingual Spanish speaker who lives in Mexico City. Only occasionally does the Angel of Vengeance sprinkle her English phrases with Spanish words like *comprende*. And, in this modification, the camera's lighting and the makeup and the general choreographing of body movement and facial expression of the actor as the Angel of Vengeance (played by former Miss Puerto Rico Denise Quiñones) hypersexualize her. Gough and Millar lighten and sexualize Rojas and willfully displace and disconnect her from her linguistic heritage (Spanish) and Mexican culture. Even her superpowers aren't rooted south of the border; in this modification of the protean Rojas, Gough and Millar locate Smallville as the source of her powers. She's one of Smallville's Kryptonite-mutated residents otherwise known as a meteor freak. So while Gough and Millar think to write a Latina into the *Smallville* storyworld absent of superheroes of color, in the end she's sexualized, dangerous, exotic, and short-lived. She only appears in one episode.

In the ten-year run of *Smallville*, only one other Latino superhero character appears: Jaime Reyes as Blue Beetle. When director Tom Welling, along with creators Alfred Gough and Miles Millar, invents a modified Jaime Reyes in Booster (season 10, episode 18, 2011); while not hypersexualized, he's whitened-up (played by Anglo Canadian Jaren Brandt Bartlett in brownface), linguistically assimilated (the only marker of his Latinidad is the "El Paso" written on his T-shirt), and irrational. Overcome with all variety of negative emotions, like anger and jealousy, this version of Jaime Reyes lets the scarab and Blue Beetle exoskeleton control him, until, that is, the Anglo golden boy Booster Gold (Eric Martsolf) arrives on the scene. The Anglo savior teaches the out-of-control, hot-tempered Latino Jaime to use reason and self-control and thus come into his own as the new Blue Beetle.

Since *Smallville*, the CW Television Network, along with others like CBS, has created several popular superhero shows, none of which feature Latinos. I think readily of Greg Berlanti and Andrew Kreisberg's *Supergirl* (CBS, 2015–) and also their *Legends of Tomorrow* (CW, 2016–). While this televisual modification of

Metropolis is absent of Latinos, the creators of *Legends of Tomorrow* do think to present a contemporary iteration of Hawkgirl as half-Latina; while Hawkgirl has been around in the DC universe from the Golden Age through to today, it was in the New 52 relaunch in 2011 that she appears as Karen Munoz-Saunders on Earth-2. To Berlanti and Kreisberg's credit, as Hawkgirl in *Legends* (as well as her cameos in *The Flash*, season 1, episode 23, and season 2, episodes 7 and 28, for instance) they cast the visibly mixed Afrolatina actor Ciara Renée as Kendra Saunders; that she speaks with a slight trace of a Nuyorican cadence grounds her in a Latina identity. However, because the televisual re-creators choose to follow her in-print comic origin story as the reincarnation of an Egyptian high priestess, the don't write into her character a backstory that would strengthen the presence of her Latinaness. In contrast, I think of other TV shows that have systematically re-racialized Latino as as African American. For instance, Félix Enríquez Alcalá's 1997 TV pilot, *Justice League of America*, features the African American actress Michelle Hurd as the Latina superhero Fire. So while Berlanti and Kreisberg don't rewrite Kendra Saunders's backstory to be Latina inclusive, they do choose to emphasize certain identity markers (linguistic and phenotypic) that guide audiences to gap-fill Hawkgirl as Latina.

These are but a few examples of televisual modifications of in-print protoworlds that feature Latinx superheroes that erase (completely absent or Anglo actors in brownface), assimilate, sexualize, and re-racialize Latinoness as visible only through a black/white racial paradigm. There are other TV modifications that evince a greater will to style and responsibility to subject matter. For instance, in the Netflix-created *Daredevil* (2015), creator Drew Goddard and his team of writers do make an effort to re-create a version of the in-print comic book character Night Nurse as the Nuyorican Latina Claire Temple (played by Puerto Rican/Cuban Rosario Dawson). Yet, the creative team misses another important opportunity when it fails to include one of Marvel's most interesting superheroes, the deaf mestizo Maya Lopez as Echo. While Cheo Coker does an incredible job at bringing fresh and alive a near-total cast of African Americans in *Luke Cage* (2016), Coker and his creative team subdue Hernán "Shades" Alvarez's Latinidad. In the writing (he's simply a Harlem gangster) and the casting

(Theo Rossi's an Italian American) the audience has no idea that Shades is Latino. And, oddly, given Netflix's better-than-average track record with televisual distillations and re-creations of Latinos in Marvel superhero storyworlds, in Melissa Rosenberg's *Jessica Jones* (2015) Latinos don't even make it to the urban backdrops of Hell's Kitchen—an urban space today where Puerto Rican Latinos make up a third of the population.

Joss Whedon and his creative team begin to do draw more deeply from the well of Latinx superheroes in their modification of the Marvel universe, *Agents of S.H.I.E.L.D.* (2013–). In ABC's season 1 of the show, it's business as usual. While clearly set in our contemporary moment, Latinos are largely absent from the story-world. When Latinos do appear, they are located south of the border as angry rebels or as the military. In season 1, for instance, the show takes audiences into the Peruvian jungle, where they encounter the Latina Comandante Camilla Reyes (played by Leonor Varela), who speaks an exaggerated accented English attempting to squash a rebel uprising. Even within this role, however, the show is less interested in portraying her as a skilled commander of armies and more as a sexed-up love interest to Anglo Agent Coulson.

As *Agents of S.H.I.E.L.D.* unfolds over the seasons, Whedon and his creative team do begin to write into the storyworld modified in-print Latinx superheroes who are complex and who stick around. For instance, in season 3, episode 11, "Bouncing Back," the story line once again travels south of the U.S.-Mexico border to Bogotá, Colombia, but this time to meet the Latina superhero Elena "Yo-Yo" Rodriguez (played by Natalia Cordova-Buckley). Yo-Yo (also known in the in-print comic as Slingshot) is street-smart, independent, and a metahuman; she can move at super speeds for the duration of one heartbeat. Yo-Yo is the central pro-tagonist of a six-part digital series, *Agents of S.H.I.E.L.D.: Slingshot* (ABC, December 13, 2016).

The six webisodes that make up *Slingshot* function as "expan-sions" of in-print comics as well as "transpositions" that enlarge the protoworld of *Agents of S.H.I.E.L.D.* These six short episodes (three to five minutes long) expand the *Agents of S.H.I.E.L.D.* storyworld and also give the Latina superhero Yo-Yo more narra-tive space. She becomes more than just a superhero warrior. She's smart and self-aware as a Latina. In the first webisode, "Vendetta,"

Figure 82. Yo-Yo Rodriguez, comic book superhero and in *Agents of S.H.I.E.L.D.*

after Coulson tells her that by signing on as an agent of S.H.I.E.L.D. she can't go directly after Ramon, the thug who killed her cousin, she remarks: "I thought America was all about freedom. When I use my powers it should be my choice." In a remarkable moment for mainstream writing of Latinas, she expresses concern that America (S.H.I.E.L.D. agency as a kind of microcosm and stand-in for U.S. America) limits her own agency. In the webisode "John Hancock," the writers poke fun at the Anglo misconception that Latino/as don't speak English. The new director of S.H.I.E.L.D. sweats it up trying to speak Spanish to Yo-Yo when she interrupts him with a furrowed brow and "English is fine." She signs on to be an agent, then summarily asks to go after the killer of her cousin ("escaped convict and arms dealer"), and Mace tells her to submit a "detailed threat assessment." She looks baffled, responding, "Submit a what now?" And, in "Progress," the interracial romance between Yo-Yo and Alphonso "Mack" Mackenzie (played by Henry Simmons) develops, even showing a kiss between a Latina and an African American. (Their interracial romance makes it once again onto the prime-time spot in season 4, episode 8, "Laws of Inferno Dynamics," when we see them kissing.) In "Reunion," when Asian American agent Melinda Qiaolian May (played by Ming-Na Wen) interrogates Yo-Yo for having stolen Director Mace's credentials, she responds, "So, you single me out because I'm the only inhuman on the base," asking the webisode audience to think about how Latinos/as are treated with suspicion as the norm in society. And in the final webisode, "Justicia," there is nearly as much Spanish spoken as English.

It seems that Whedon and his creative team are not just modifying and expanding protean in-print Latinx superheroes within the webisode margins. With season 4 they cast Latino actor Gabriel Luna as Marvel's new Ghost Rider, Robbie Reyes. And, they cast Latino actor Lorenzo James Henrie in their modified re-creation of Robbie's younger brother, Gabe. This move to follow the continuity of Marvel's *All-New Ghost Rider* series (2014–) and not the Anglo Johnny Blaze's story line met with some controversy and pushback by some Marvel fans. Needless to say, that Whedon and his creative team made this significant move is a big step forward for Latinx superheroes on mainstream TV. The creators follow the comic book in that they create a balanced representation of Latinos from East L.A.: Robbie code-switches English and Spanish, is street-smart, and makes money through illegal street races. While Robbie is the primary caregiver to the younger brother, Gabe, Whedon and his team move away from the in-print comic with Gabe's characterization. In the comic, Gabe is born with no motor control of his legs (his mother's fall during pregnancy) and is a preteen. For the TV show re-creation, they invent Gabe as a late teen, wise beyond his years, pensive, and well on his way to a place like Stanford with his book smarts.

In season 4, episode 6, "The Good Samaritan," the audience learns that it's Robbie's ties to the gang world that leads to Gabe being shot and paralyzed. While the creators of *Agents of S.H.I.E.L.D.* ask the audience not to sympathize with Robbie, later the show does ask us to sympathize when we learn that Robbie sold his soul to the Spirit of Vengeance to save Gabe's life. Not only does the show deliver complex Latinos, but it's a show that's aware of how Latinos

Figure 83. Robbie Reyes in *Agents of S.H.I.E.L.D.* and as comic book character.

are stereotyped in the mainstream. When Robbie's put on Director Mace's radar, he calls him a terrorist, to which Agent Coulson responds, "It's a bit Fox News to call him a terrorist." And when Robbie takes down his maligned genius, *tío* Eli Morrow (played by José Zúñiga), the creators give Eli enough of a backstory for us to understand why he's become hungry for the Darkhold's power. He spent a lifetime being told he was never good enough by the *gūeros*, or fair-skinned ones. That is to say, between the two of them we see the creation of characters that present a complex spectrum of what it means to be Latino.

ABC is not alone in this double move (TV and web platforms) to modify and re-create in-print Latino superheroes. With *The Flash* (2014–), CW's creative team Greg Berlanti, Andrew Kreisberg, and Geoff Johns choose to cast Latino Carlos Valdez as Cisco Ramon. They also create him as a central character, even if an Anglo (Barry Allen) still gets the lead as the Flash. And while the creators write Cisco as a bit of the comedic relief, he's not a buffoon. He's filled with quick, witty replies. And he's less identified by his body (recall his break-dance in-print 1980s incarnation) and more his mind. He's a super genius engineer and tech wiz. And, while the writers of the show have him often functioning as Barry Allen's brown nurturer—he's a kind of in-house nurse— he stands his ground when Barry crosses lines. For instance, when Barry selfishly changes the narrative timeline in order to live a happy life complete with girlfriend, Iris West, and a living mother, he inadvertently kills off Cisco's brother, Dante Ramon (played by Nicholas Gonzalez) (season 3, episode 1, "Flashpoint"). Once Cisco learns that that Barry's changing of the timeline caused the death of Dante, he puts Barry at an emotional arm's length (season 3, episode 7, "Killer Frost," and episode 8, "Invasion.")

As seen with the complicating of Latinoness with Yo-Yo and her digital presence on the web, so, too, do we see this with Cisco. On April 19, 2016, four webisodes appeared, titled "The Chronicles of Cisco." In the short one-to-two-minute story lines we meet Cisco working out how to create a bulletproof Flash suit, not only expanding what we see in *The Flash*, season 2, but also providing more depth of character in Cisco. He's the protagonist. He's the main subject problem solving and experiencing important emotions in and around the appearance of Shawna Baez as Peek-a-Boo (played by African Canadian Britne Oldford). Barry Allen is nowhere to be seen. And, the creators are careful to be sure that the audience sees on Cisco's work desk the special glasses that harness his brain waves and allow him to vision quest when wearing them. As the fourth webisode concludes, we're not sure if this was all Cisco's dream, or if it all actually happened, but he does solve the problem of how to make Barry's suit bulletproof. Notably, too, Cisco's given additional breadth and agency through his blog, "The Chronicles of Cisco," where, for instance, it's not Barry Allen who is calling the shots, but a smart, witty, feisty Cisco. He introduces himself as: "Just your average, run-of-the-mill mechanical engineering super-genius with super powers. Yeah, one day the world will know me as Vibe but for now, I keep it real working with my team to keep the streets of Central City safe. Oh, who's on my team? The Flash. Yeah, that's my boy. Together, we're kicking ass and taking names one metahuman at a time" (http://chroniclesofcisco.tumblr.com/).

Digital platforms have expanded the storyworld universes of two prime-time shows. And they have done so in their willful complication and enlargement of the creator's modified in-print Latino/a superheroes.

At the very least, CW and ABC seem attuned to the fact that audiences of their shows are racially diverse—and Latinx. The superhero storyworlds re-created by Fox's different teams seem to fall short in their televisual modifications of Latinx superheroes. In the Batman spinoff, *Gotham* (2014–), there is one recurring Latino character, Detective Carlos Alvarez (played by Nuyorican J. W. Cortés). That the creators of *Gotham* give this minor character in the comic book world (*Catwoman*, vol. 4, #4) some level of prominence and screen time in the series is perhaps encouraging. However, in the end what Fox feeds its viewers is yet another Latino relegated to the stereotypical; in this case, it's the disgruntled urban cop and not the drug kingpin or the sexed-up military commander. And, given that the setting is a recognizable distillation and reconstruction of a U.S. society, that Latinos are absent from all other parts of the show is remarkable.

Televisual modifications of protoworlds from the DC and Marvel in-print universe are not only the repository for the creating of superhero storyworlds inclusive of Latinos. Those like James Cameron with his *Dark Angel* (2000–2002) simply choose to re-create from the building blocks of an increasingly diverse U.S. reality. Cameron and his creative team cast Latina Jessica Alba to play the role of his multiethnic superhero, Maxine "Max" Guevara. They write her character as smart, super strong, and with a deeply humanitarian impulse. Max saves the vulnerable and the persecuted (outcast metahumans) in a post-apocalyptic Seattle. Cameron and his creative team clearly aim to build a storyworld that complicates identity on all levels, including gender, race, ethnicity, and class. Max, along with the other young mixed-race women (straight and gay) we meet in the show, is filled with agency. The show depicts all kinds of same-sex and heterosexual romances, and between all variety of different races and ethnicities. And, the show does its best not to heterosexualize Max as the Latina superhero. She's portrayed more as androgynous tomboy (in outfits and her day-time occupation as bike messenger) than sexy, spandexed superhero. The creators build her relationship with her best friend, Original Cindy (played by Valerie Rae Miller), who is simply an out lesbian.

Figure 84. Max with Original Cindy in *Dark Angel,* "Pilot."

When Max does have a love interest, she's not depicted as a sexual appendage but as intellectual equal. (Cameron and his creative team also destabilize the traditional Anglo patriarch by creating her love interest, Logan Cale, as differently abled and an activist vigilante.) Max is the product of Project Chimera, where she and twelve other orphans (twelve has a clear biblical reference) with recombinative DNA become physically and mentally superhuman. Finally, Max's education or bildungsroman leads her from acting alone as superhero to heal the shorn social tissue to working in solidarity with a collective of metahumans and humans. In Cuban Latino Reneé Echevaría's produced grand finale, "Freak Nation" (May 2012), to the series, Max stands alongside other transgenics (hybrid, interspecies subjects discriminated against by the humans) and declares: "We were made in America and we are not going anywhere. Who is with me?" The outcast transgenics stand in solidarity with metahuman Max, holding their fists of power high in the air as the militarized police as appendage of the state apparatus back away. Cameron and his creative team's distillation and reconstruction of our contemporary reality with all variety of ambiguous racial, ethnic, and sexual identities function to destabilize exclusionary ideologies: who belongs and doesn't belong within the nation state.

There are other televisual superhero storyworlds that seek to distill and re-create from the ethnic diversity that makes up our contemporary U.S. reality. For instance, while Tim Kring's *Heroes* (NBC, 2006–2010) does invent a panoply of mostly Anglo superheroes (cheerleader, politician, wealthy matriarch, police officer), it includes superheroes from Asia as well as African American D. L. Hawkins and mixed-race Micha Sanders—*and* Latino artist, comic book author, and visionary Isaac Méndez (played by Santiago Cabrera). Adilifu Nama remarks on how the show's writing of diversity into its story line was "fresh and truly provocative" (146). As the series developed, the creative team continued to create Latinx superheroes, but as with Isaac Méndez, the show would kill them off. For instance, in season 2, episode 1, "Four Months Later . . ." (2007) the show's creative team invents two new Latino characters: the Dominican Republic–origined, monolingual Spanish-speaking super twins Maya Herrera (played by Dania Ramirez) and Alejandro Herrera (played by Shalom Ortiz). Extreme duress triggers Maya's superpower: the lethal poisoning of anyone in her proximity. Alejandro's superpower: to counteract and deactivate his sister's lethal superpower. Before the narrative has the supervillain Sylar kill them off, we see them crossing borders (Honduras/Guatemala/Mexico/U.S.). In the border crossing scene at the U.S.-Mexico border, a super anxious and stressed Maya releases her power: her eyes turn black and she induces the poisoning death of an armed mercenary gang of Anglos known as Citizens Border Patrol.

In 2015 Tim Kring expanded the storyworld of superhumans (EVOs) in digital platform and NBC primetime. With the web-based six-chapter series *Dark Matters* (July 9, 2015) audiences learn that the EVOs are now nearly everywhere, including south of the border and as U.S. Latinos. However, director Tanner Kring and writer Zach Craley choose to follow (handheld documentary-style) the everyday life of Anglo Phoebe Johnson (she can steal light and channel darkness) as she moves into her college dorm and meets her roommate, Aly (played by Russian Nigerian Greta Onieogou)—a regular human of color (webisode 2); as she registers with a fed-eral database as an evolved human—the creators purposely build a mise-en-scène to look like an INS inscription office (webisode 3); during her disappearance and then supposed involvement in a "terrorist" attack (webisode 4); and during her brother Quintin's rendezvous with Micha Sanders, now grown up and known as Hero Truther (played by African American Noah Gray-Cabey), the organizer of the EVO resistance. The webisodes function as a back-story and continuity story line (Phoebe and her brother, Quentin, both reappear as characters) between the original *Heroes* and Tim

Figure 85. El Vengador in *Heroes: Reborn*, "The Lion's Den" (October 15, 2015).

Kring's miniseries reboot, *Heroes: Reborn*, that aired on NBC a few months after the *Dark Matters* webisodes appeared. In *Heroes: Reborn* Kring invents a Latino superhero who is one of the central protagonists: El Vengador as the L.A.-based, ex-military Catholic Carlos Gutierrez (played by Ryan Guzman). Carlos assumes the superhero identity of his murdered brother, Oscar Gutierrez (played by Marco Grazzini).

Figure 86. El Vengador in the comic book *Heroes: Vengeance* (2016).

Unlike the other Latino characters who appeared in *Heroes*, Carlos is not associated with drugs (Isaac's a heroin addict), crossing borders without documents, or criminal activities generally. And, he's not killed off within an episode or two. Indeed, Kring creates a Latino who is deeply empathetic and invested with great powers of reason and superhuman strength. Carlos appears throughout the thirteen episodes that make up the miniseries; other Latinos appear throughout the show, including Carlos's nephew, Jose Gutierrez (played by Lucius Hoyos), and Carlos's priest and confidant, the smoke shifter Father Mauricio (Carlos LaCamara). And, with Seamus Kevin Fahey and Zach Craley (writers) and Rubine (artist) creation of *Heroes: Vengeance*, "El Vengador" (2016), Carlos's characterization expands within the graphic novel *Heroes: Reborn* universe.

While the digital webisode platform features Anglos, we see with the televisual and graphic novel storyworlds of *Heroes: Reborn* the creation of a superhero space actively inclusive of Latinos. We see a distillation and reconstruction of our U.S. Latinx reality. This re-creation with Latinos front and center is less the case with the expansions, modifications, and transpositions that take place in the making of silver screen comic book superheroes.

Silver Screened Super Browns

Beginning in the 1990s and in full swing in the 2000s, in-print comic book superheroes made their way onto the silver screen in increased number and with increased frequency. The abundance of filmic versions encapsulated the wide spectrum of transmedial expansions, modifications, and transpositions. While some were done to better effect than others (Tim Burton's versus Joel Schumacher's transpositions of Batman and Gotham, for instance), overall they became a cash cow for Hollywood. They also grew to dominate their in-print comic book protoworld kin. By 2012, hundreds of films had been re-created from in-print comic books and comic strips and with massive profits made. (For more on this, see Henry Pratt, "Making Comics into Film.") And yet, in spite of their omnipresence and go-anywhere CGI technological wizardry whereby audiences can be transported to Krypton, Asgard, Ryut, and Xander, filmic re-creations of superhero comics remain willfully ignorant of their own sublunary subjects: Latinos. Latinos are either erased altogether or hyperpresent as super-sexualized, criminalized, or moronic subjects. And when silver screen superhero storyworlds include Latino-marked spaces (Mexico, Puerto Rico, Central or South America) they are either frozen in some pre-Columbian mystical past, or filled to the brim with violence.

There are less than a handful of directors who choose to re-create superhero comic book films inclusive of Latinas generally. When Latinas are present, they appear as hypersexualized accoutrements to the Anglo protagonists. Mark Steven Johnson's *Ghost Rider* (2007) is a case in point. *Ghost Rider* opens with a shot that establishes the story somewhere in a Spanish colonial-style northern Mexican town; the Caretaker (voiced by Sam Elliot) identifies this as San Venganza, where the legend of the Ghost Rider begins. Mexico (actual filming took place in Australia) is frozen in some bygone past. It's also the place where the Ghost Rider refuses to sign on the dotted line with Mephistopheles (Peter Fonda) to become all-powerful, helping to create a literal hell on earth. Here already we see a common trope among comic book films: the physical space of Latinoness existing in the past and the fantastical. When the story proper begins, we're in the same arid landscape, but somewhere in the U.S. Southwest—Mexican northern territories prior to the signing of the 1848 Treaty of Guadalupe. It's a world with few Latinos but overflowing with Anglos, including the protagonist, Johnny Blaze (played by Nicholas Cage). The Latina who does appear is Blaze's love-interest, Roxanne "Roxy" Simpson (Eva Mendes); with the exception of one homeless guy (Estefanie Sousa), she's the only visible marker of Latinoness in this contemporary Southwest.

Johnson's *Ghost Rider* makes it clear that he and his creative team aren't interested in distilling and reconstructing from a Southwest reality that's Latino-majority. Indeed, there's a near total absence of Latinos. The one Latina who does appear is scripted, dressed, and made up as a sexed-up brown body. After the requisite hot and steamy scenes between Simpson and Blaze, Simpson is given little screen time, reappearing only at the film's denouement among the ruins of San Venganza: she's less smart/ruthless warrior and more slinky sex kitten, hanging off the shoulder of her Anglo protector as he saves the world from evil.

Freezing Latinoness in bygone times or its hypersexual presence in the form of Latina love interests are recurring strategies in superhero comic book films, and this across all the genres, the

Figure 87. Eva Mendes as Roxanne "Roxy" Simpson in *Ghost Rider* (2007).

Figure 88. Nicholas Cage as Ghost Rider, saving the world from evil in *Ghost Rider* (2007).

western included. In *Jonah Hex* (2010), the superhero western, director Jimmy Hayward, along with writers Mark Neveldine and Brian Taylor, chooses to re-create and modify the in-print comic book Anglo superhero cowboy Jonah Hex (played by Josh Brolin). In their filmic modification and expansion of the Jonah Hex character, they put an emphasis on his resurrection and vision quest under the guidance of a Native American Crow tribal shaman. He returns to life to avenge the deaths of his son and wife, both phenotypically identifiable as mestizo. This filmic re-creation buries the in-print comic book Hex's indigenous backstory (his father sold him to an Apache tribe, which raised him) and focuses instead on the singular drive of a flawed, socially alienated, monstrous (half-burned face and undead) Hex to avenge his family's death. The film creator's modification provides little reason why the Anglo Hex is resurrected by the native shaman or why he's with his Native American family. Hex's story comes off as yet another *Dances with Wolves*, white savior narrative. And, the modification that takes place with the casting of actors also falls short. They choose to cast mixed Asian/Anglo American Moon Bloodgood as Hex's Sioux wife, Tallbird.

Figure 89. Tallbird in the original comic, and Moon Bloodgood as Tallbird in the film *Jonah Hex* (2010).

And, in the re-creation of another of the indigenous characters that appear in the in-print comic, Tallulah Black, Hayward and his creative team choose Megan Fox in brownface. Their modification erases Tallulah's indigeneity as well as her backstory, in which she is a rape victim left for dead, with facial scars and a dislodged eye. The filmic modification leaves on the cutting room floor, too, her resurgence in the comic book as a kick-ass, sharpshooting bounty hunter. Hayward and his creative team choose to erase indigeneity (a nonindigenous actress to play Tallbird) and a differently abled female with agency (Fox in brownface). (Notably, this modification also happens in Gavin Hood's *Wolverine* (2009), where blue-eyed Lynn Collins is cast to play Wolverine's indigenous love-interest, Kayla Silver Fox.)

Figure 90. Tallulah as comic book character and Megan Fox as Tallulah in the film *Jonah Hex* (2010).

Latinos as sexualized objects, seed for Anglo vengeance plots, or healers of Anglo superheroes are commonplace themes in filmic re-creations. So, too, are certain locations, such as the gritty urban, the arid rural, or the hot tropical. In *The Punisher* (2004) director Jonathan Hensleigh chooses to modify the comic book protoworld setting of Frank Castle's transformation into the vigilante known as the Punisher from Central Park to the tropical, Aguadilla Bay, Puerto Rico. This becomes the site where former undercover FBI agent and Delta Force soldier Frank Castle (played by Thomas Jane) loses his entire family; they're all murdered by the drug kingpin Howard Saint (played by John Travolta). In this filmic modification, Hensleigh makes Latinoness as identified by geographic place the space of white superhero resurrection. After the mob murders Castle's family and blows him up, he's fished out of the water by the Afrolatino houngun (healer) Candelaria (played by Veryl Jones). Candelaria performs some mystical healing (Vodun?) practices and

Castle comes back from the dead. In this re-creation, Latinoness is location (the tropical) and the mystical (Afrolatino houngun ritual). It's also the violent and salacious. Hensleigh includes two Latinos, the Toro brothers (played by Omar Avila and Eduardo Yáñez), and creates a backstory for Howard Saint's wife, Olivia, that portrays her as a former prostitute from Miami's Little Cuba.

Pitof's *Catwoman* (2004) embodies this move to hypersexualize and geographically locate Latinoness in the re-creation and modification of comic book superheroes. Director Pitof and his creative team do a great job casting an actual Latino actor to play the Latino love interest and detective, Tom Lone (played by Benjamin Bratt). There is also clearly a will to style involved in the film's casting of the racially ambiguous Halle Berry as artist-by-day Patience Phillips, and Catwoman by night. However, rather than fully modify Catwoman as, say, fully Afrolatina, by identifying her origins as, say, Puerto Rican, Dominican, or Cuban, the film simply wants the audience to read her as urban and ambiguously multiethnic. And Pitof chooses to foreground the "ethnicity" of Lone and Phillips when they are shooting hoops in the inner city and suddenly can't control their *animal* attraction. They are choreographed to play basketball as an exchange of booty grinds—all while a ragtag group of multiethnic youngsters cheers them on. When they are "ethnic," they *are* urban and hypersexual.

Pitof's casting of the Latino Bratt is not the last time we see him appear in a superhero film. Indeed, in *Dr. Strange* (2016) Ben Scott Derrickson invents an entirely new character in the Marvel studio universe: Jonathan Pangborn—played by Bratt—a factory worker turned paraplegic who trains with The Ancient One at Kamar-Taj in Kathmandu, Nepal, to become a protector of the Sanctums. However, rather than choose to use his mystical powers as guardian, Pangborn uses them to walk again and to return to New York. Like Tom Lone in *Catwoman*, the Latino is identified as street-urban. When Dr. Strange searches for Pangborn to discover how he is able to walk again, Pangborn is shooting hoops. In so many words, Derrickson, along with co-writers Jon Spaihts and C. Robert Cargill, writes a Latino character into the film that we've seen before: a person who is not to be trusted *and* who only appears for a brief couple of minutes, and this includes a flash of an instant in a post-post-credit scene when Derrickson chooses to show him working with tools in a mechanics workshop being drained of his powers by one of the few other racially marked characters in the film, Karl Mordo (Chiwetel Ejiofor), which leaves him paralyzed once again.

Figure 91. Patience Phillips/Catwoman (Halle Berry) and Tom Lone (Benjamin Bratt) in Pitof's *Catwoman* (2004).

Following a long tradition of Hollywood's lazy and prejudiced representations of Latinos, those who appear in comic book superhero films often also exist as fixed in time and place: in a distant past (a Spanish colonial village) and/or in a desert, exotic landscape, or urban location. We see various combinations of this fixing of Latinoness even in films with a greater will to center-stage race. I think of those comic book superhero films that seek to right representational wrongs when it comes to African Americans. Time and again we see even these films slipping into clichés about Latinos.

For instance, while Kenneth Johnson's *Steel* (1997) broke new ground in its creation of an African American protagonist, Steel, played by Shaquille "Shaq" O'Neal, it joins the trend of such films as, for example, *The Meteor Man* (1993), *Spawn* (1997), and *Blade* (1998), in which Latinos are present but only as violent and idiotic gangbangers. Latinos for Anglo director Kenneth Johnson seem to be either fixed permanently in time and place—*Steel* opens with the military testing a new superweapon in a Mexican colonial village (again?)—or thick-accented English-speaking, bandana-wearing, gun-wielding gangsters cruising for trouble in their Buick lowrider.

As superhero films reach for our stars and beyond, they spend more and more money on special effects, millions upon millions of dollars to create immersive simulacra of otherworldly spaces. Yet it seems that with this increasing expenditure to bring to life otherworldly spaces and beings there's a simultaneous willful absenting of Latinos. For instance, in making *Green Lantern* (2011) Martin Campbell could have chosen as his Green Lantern the half-Mexican Kyle Rayner; as mentioned in the first chapter of this book, "Rayner" was the invented alias of Kyle's Mexican father, Gabriel Vasquez, who worked as an operative for the CIA. Instead, Campbell and his fellow creators (writers Greg Berlanti, Michael Green, and Marc Guggenheim) choose as their protagonist the Anglo Green Lantern Hal Jordan (played by Ryan Reynolds). They do re-create otherness in the story line, but it's not Latino, African American (the 1970s John Stewart as Green Lantern), or queer (Judd Winick's 2001 creation of a gay assistant to Rayner). Otherness in the film comes in the form of the exotic: Jewish Maori actor Taika Waititi as Jordan's Inuit engineer at Ferris Aircraft, and New Zealand Maori actor Temuera Morrison as Hal Jordan's outer galaxy predecessor, Abin Sur, from planet Ungara. Campell et al. choose to re-create otherness as safely contained within the distant and exotic; as with so many Hollywood films, racial otherness is present but at a safe distance—in this case, the distance of galaxies.

In 2016, when David Ayer brought to the silver screen the ragtag team of supervillains-cum-reluctant-superheroes with *Suicide Squad,* he also center-staged for the first time in DC's film history a Latino superhero: a tattooed Jay Hernandez plays Chato Santana as El Diablo. While Ayer (director and writer) gestures toward creating him as one of the more sympathetic supercriminals of the

Figure 92. Maori actor Temuera Morrison.

bunch—he's given *some* cinematic space to share his grief at the loss of his wife and two children—he fails to live up to the ethical complexity of his characterization in the pre–New 52 and New 52 in-print comic book iterations. (Unlike in the earlier iterations, in the New 52 reboot Chato is tattooed and without a demonic horse, a fiery whip, and most of his clothing.) In *Suicide Squad*, vol. 1, "Kicked in the Teeth" (2012), writer Adam Glass and artist Federico Dallacchio invest Santana as El Diablo with greater richness and complexity, giving him more space to develop his deep conflicts over being a gangbanger, to repent and struggle with past misdeeds, like his murder of innocent women and children.

Ayer does bring some of this conflict into his on-screen re-creation of Santana as El Diablo. When Santana tells his story at a bar, Ayer builds into the film a flashback that conveys this sense of the source of his conflict. The audience doesn't see him burning

Figure 93. Temuera Morrison as Abin Sur in *Green Lantern* (2011).

Figure 94. Chato Santana as El Diablo in *Suicide Squad*, vol. 1, "Kicked in the Teeth" (2012).

anonymous innocents as in the comic. Rather, it shows him at home with his wife, Grace (played by Corina Calderon), and children; Ayer portrays Santana and Grace in hypersexualized ways: during a breakfast scene she sports a low-cut tank-top and short shorts and he can't resist slapping her derrière.

Figure 95. Chato at home with family in *Suicide Squad* (2016).

Ayer's backstory does present the source of Santana's grief. Grace confronts Santana over his stash of guns and cash: "This is our home. I'm taking my kids to mom's." Santana loses his temper, then Ayer cuts to a scene where Santana is holding his dead wife in an incinerated house. With a cut to the present, Santana tells the rest of the suicide squad: "When I get mad I lose control." Certainly, Ayer creates a conflict born of personal tragedy, but ultimately one that characterizes the Latino superhero as so out-of-control tempestuous that he murders his own family. The flashback ends. Filled with grief, Santana remarks, "I don't know what I do till it's done."

But this fleshing out of Santana doesn't come until the story's denouement in the film's final thirty-eight minutes. In contrast with the other superhero mercenaries who are fleshed out at the beginning of the film, it takes twenty-four minutes of film time before Ayer introduces Santana as Diablo: "I'm a man, not a weapon. I'm gonna die in peace before I raise my fists again," he tells the Anglo leader of the squad, Rick Flag (played by Joel Kinnaman). Up until the midpoint in the film, Santana is largely silent. Ayer includes in Santana's script the occasional interjection of words like "homie" and "ese." The choice of his theme music (WAR's "Slippin' into Darkness"), his tank top and Ben Sherman pants, and the random assortment of body, head, and face tattoos—"Diablo," "Muerte," "Familia," "Mi Vida Loca," and "Hill Side" images of the Virgin de Guadalupe, a tear drop, and the number "MS13" on the back of his shaved head to indicate that he's a member of the Mara Salvatrucha, or MS13—function as other identifiers of his Cholo barrio origins and Latino identity, but as a gangbanger. To Ayer's credit, Santana is ultimately written as the only repentant superhero—and with this, he has a sense of right and wrong that his fellow Suicide Squad members do not. And, in the end, he's the character who ends up willing to sacrifice himself for the greater good. To save the other members of the squad and humanity generally, he declares, "I lost one family. I ain't gonna lose another. I got this. Let me show you what I really am." He then morphs into a giant fireball, and oddly, sporting a loincloth and some kind of feathered headdress. After he announces "te chingaste, güay!" he attempts to take down loincloth-wearing (the Mesoamerican look) Dr. June Moone as Enchantress (played by Cara Delevingne) and her supervillain brother, The Incubus (played by Alain Chanoine), but it's ultimately the other members of the Suicide Squad who save the day.

Certainly, Ayer and his creative team are careful to re-create the in-print comic book superhero Santana's metahuman power, his pyro-rages. However, by choosing to show him killing his own family (not in the comic book original) when he plays the part of the repentant gangbanger, it falls short. And, of course, when he flips to become the one who saves the day through self sacrifice, again he plays to all the stereotypes: Latinos as either hot-headed murderers or as sacrificial lambs. We might excuse this as part of Ayer's creative license. However, when El Diablo is the only Latino to make it from the mainstream in-print comics to the silver screen in any substantive way, he carries much representational weight. So, when Ayer and his creative team choose to re-create him as murderer of his own family *and* collapse all variety of Mesoamerican historical religious ceremonial practice into one big blend, we see once again a missed opportunity and a lack of a clear will to shape and style Latinoness with greater complexity. Finally, we have to consider Ayer's choice to create the antagonist, Dr. June Moone turned into Enchantress, as a throwback to a Latin American primitivism. We see Dr. Moone exploring pyramids in a tropical (South American) jungle, where she's inhabited by the mystical powers of a pre-Columbian metahuman *bruja*. Once transformed, Dr. Moone's skin turns from pearly white to tattooed charcoal black and sepia-hued brown, and with a loincloth and crescent moon headgear. And with this we see those age-old clichés surface once again. When the spirit of Enchantress (indigeneity) inhabits Dr. Moon (whiteness) she becomes dangerous— globally destructive dangerous—turning civilians (with a kiss) into *blackened* monstrous henchmen, known as Eyes of the Adversary, who wear military gear over a crusty epidermis that's pustulating goo in and around a multitude of black eyeballs. Once the squad takes her down (with Santana's ultimate self-sacrifice), Dr. Moone emerges once again from a black epidermis–encased Enchantress. White emerges from dark, Anglo from a Latin American–located dark and dangerous indigeneity.

With other comic book films we witness different degrees of a willful erasure of Latinos. In Zack Snyder's *Batman v. Superman: Dawn of Justice* (2016) Latinos are present, but only as one TV news reporter (a cameo by the actual newscaster Soledad O'Brien) and a population that worships the white Anglo savior Superman. In a film where Superman (played by British actor Henry Cavill) has just saved Metropolis from a high-tech alien takeover lead by General Zod, Snyder and writers Chris Terrio and David S. Goyer have him speed across the U.S.-Mexico border to Ciudad Juárez to save a girl from a burning building. The narrative not only portrays Mexicans as in need of saving from a relatively banal event (in comparison to the high-tech alien invasion), but also it just so happens that the rescue takes place on *Día de los Muertos*. Most of the Latinos seen are in *calavera* makeup. In this filmic distillation and reconstruction of a contemporary America, Latino characters appear once in the United States (O'Brien) and as a mass of people desperately in *need* of saving, primed for white superhero (messianic) worship—and indulgent in pagan ("primitivist") ritual. Indeed, like many Marvel and DC films today, Zachary Snyder's Superman functions as an alternative fantasy of white masculinity saving the world from another 9/11 "terrorist" attack in order to reassert the relevance of this subjectivity—but as a marginalized subjectivity. As Jeffrey A. Brown states generally of today's filmic Supermans, Batmans, Deadpools, and Spideys, with "the increased visibility and awareness of identity politics [we see] a different approach to the reaffirmation of white masculinity taking place in superhero movies that includes incorporating a form of marginalization into the character in order to then redeem him" (*The Modern Superhero in Film and Television*, e-book). With Snyder's Superman shunned by working-class U.S. men like out-of-work and disabled Wallace Keefe and adored by powerless Latinos, Snyder reaffirms white masculinity's mythic centrality in and across careless reconstructions of the Latino margins.

Figure 96. Anglo savior Superman worshipped by Mexicans in Zack Snyder's *Batman v. Superman: Dawn of Justice* (2016).

In *Thor* (2011) we see a greater degree of this willful erasure of Latinos. British director Kenneth Branagh sliced out the only sequence in the film that included Latinos—and this in a film where the action takes place largely in a contemporary town called Puente Antigua in New Mexico. Most would know that New Mexico is majority Latino. In any re-creation, the building blocks of the social landscape a director like Branagh would be using would be Latino. Instead, the film literally cuts out the footage that had Latinos: Adriana Barraza (typecast as the maid or undocumented nanny in films) as Isabela Alvarez, the town's café owner, *serving*

Thor some coffee followed by Latinx children playing in the street. With its near two-hour run time, the film features *one* Latinx: a Latina nurse appears in the opening scenes when Thor is admitted to a hospital. Branagh goes to great lengths to build Puente Antigua from scratch (a film set in Galisteo, New Mexico), only to then fill it to the brim with Anglo twentysomething hipsters. Of course, Branagh, or any director for that matter, is free to re-create the building blocks of reality in whatever way he or she chooses. However, when that reality is clearly one filled with Latinos—a New Mexico town—and Latinos are deliberately not chosen not to be present, then it's no longer a question of ignorance. It's the creator's will to exclude and erase.

We see this will to exclude in Christopher Nolan's modifications, expansions, and transpositions of Batman. While his Dark Knight trilogy is extraordinary in many of the ways one gives shape to a film (editing, lighting, scoring, and so on), it fails in its reconstructions of the building blocks of in-print comic books and the contemporary reality in which they are set. With *Batman Begins* (2005) Nolan reconstructs a contemporary Chicago as his Gotham. He includes a number of deliberate anachronisms, including a futuristic Wayne Enterprises high-speed train that floats over technologically sophisticated rails and carries passengers dressed as if from the 1950s. Under Nolan's deft director hand, this works to help establish an anything-goes contract with the viewer. However, that the passengers behind the Wayne family are largely Anglo (there's one well-dressed black passenger reading a paper) speaks to the will to exclude racial others here and throughout the film.

When Nolan has Bruce Wayne return to Gotham as an adult (after slumming it with lowlifes in the third world), he doesn't hide the fact that Gotham is built visually out of the building blocks of a real, contemporary Chicago, a city filled with Latinos today. Yet, in this two-hour-plus film, the only Latinos who appear are the mustachioed maître d' (David Bedella, of Mexican heritage) at the hotel Bruce procures while entertaining a gaggle of society girls that includes one with a darker phenotypic shade who might pass as Latina (played by British actress of Spanish and Italian descent Alexandra Bastedo). Of course, there is ambiguity here, too. There is ultimately not enough from the context or from what is said for us to determine absolutely that they are Latinx. They could just as well be Italian, but for Nolan that seems good enough. They certainly are not on the train that's filled with workers traveling to and from Gotham, or even in the working-class neighborhood known as the Narrows.

Arguably even more egregiously, Nolan chooses not to place a Latino center stage where he could have done so most easily and organically: in the *Dark Knight Rises* (2012). Here Nolan and David Goyer (writer) choose to cast Tom Harding as Bane, the greatest Latino supervillain in the DC universe. So instead of a smart, physically awesome Latino supervillain, we are served up Bane with an English accent muffled through his breathing mask. The opportunity to bring to life one of the great Latinx supervillains is passed over. (The choice of casting incensed the comic's fan community, with blogs and message boards filled with fans' venting over the erasure of Bane's Latino backstory.)

There are plenty of other Latino erasures and missed opportunities in comic book superhero filmmaking. For instance, director Joe Johnston and his creative team missed an excellent opportunity for writing Latinos into *Captain America* (2011) when building Cap's origin story. While many think of the Latino zoot-suiters of the 1940s as L.A.-based, they were also in Chicago, Philadelphia, *and* New York. Johnson does a good job of creating an origin story that connects a bullied, diminutive, pre-super-serumed Steve Rogers (white working class) with Jewish persecution, but given the historical fact that Latinos existed in New York (Spanish Harlem and Lower East Side, especially) and Brooklyn during this time (especially sartorially visible in their zoot suit fashionwear) as well as the huge number of U.S. Latinos fighting in World War II, a more complete backstory could have intensified Latino audience connection and engagement. This also could have been done with Johnston and his creative team weaving in more backstory to Jim Morita—the Japanese American (from Fresno) member of Cap's Howling Commandoes team—which might have provided an opportunity for the film to include (even if briefly) in its backstory the history that connects concentration camps with Japanese American internment camps, as well as this period's labor camps in California where Japanese Americans, Filipino Americans, and Mexican Americans cohabitated. Of course, these are all what-ifs, but they are pointed what-ifs, in that yet again we see a lack of will to include elements (historical facts) that might have made for a comic book film that reached a little beyond the usual white-guy savior narrative and made for a more enriching experience for Latinos and other audiences of color.

I should add briefly that while being a Latino director (and creator generally) tends to put one more directly in front of Latinx experiences that might make their way into comic book films, it's not always the case. I think readily of Guillermo del Toro and his creative team's making of *Blade II* (2002). When this came out, I thought I'd see a distillation and reconstruction in fantasy form those building blocks of reality that include Latinos. Latinos could also be in leadership positions to vampires, vampire slayers, and "Reaper" monsters. Del Toro chooses instead to cast Anglo Ron Perlman as Dieter Reinhardt, the leader of the vampire-slaying Bloodpack—a villainous team that includes one Asian character, Snowman (Donnie Yen), and one Anglo member who sports indigenous Maori tattoo body art. The presence of Latinoness comes in the dropping of the occasional Spanish word like *Jefe* and in the presence of the whimpering vampire Rush (played by Spanish actor Santiago Segura). To del Toro's credit, he does cast Chilean Leonor Varela as the "good" vampire, Nyssa. However, her gendered (and monstrous) agency quickly slips into sexualized clichés, not only in her leather get-up, but also in her *need* to be rescued by the muscled, taciturn black male protagonist, Blade (Wesley Snipes).

Given that the civil rights struggle inspired Stan Lee and Jack Kirby in the creating of Marvel's *X-Men* series, one would think that Latinos—and race more generally—would also find its way more forcefully into its film re-creations. (Most notably, perhaps, we see in the names chosen and the distinctive political visions conveyed how Malcolm X and Martin Luther King Jr. weave their way into the characterizations of Charles Xavier/Professor X and Magneto.) This is not the case.

This isn't to say that the *X-Men* films erase entirely the original comic book series' awareness of U.S. race relations. They do furnish a number of signposts that guide audiences to read the films as allegories of today's U.S. race relations, including the propaganda around undocumented Latinos. For instance, after director Bryan Singer launches *X-Men* (2000) with a prologue-like sequence set in a Warsaw concentration camp (Erik Lehnsherr as Magneto's origin story), audiences are thrown in medias res the moment Senator Robert Kelly (Bruce Davison) announces the passing of the Mutant Registration Act: to "defend" and "protect citizens" and their "God given right of free will." Clearly, Singer wants audiences to carefully consider the passing of xenophobic policy in defense of "freedom" (one that alone led to the Nazis' "ethnic cleansing" policies and the Jewish Holocaust), but also to make connections between disenfranchised (undocumented Latinos) and enfranchised (an Anglo patriarchy, represented by the composition of the U.S. Senate). As Senator Robert Kelley tells his fellow senators, the mutants move "*among us*," threatening from within U.S. borders a destruction of the American way of life.

By putting front and center the mutant question, Singer also foregrounds today's Latino question. However, when it comes to including Latinos in his contemporary U.S. films, he falls short. Singer (and other directors of the franchise) erases Latinos from his film's landscape, either by not representing them in his urban settings or by willfully not including those few Latino X-Men that populate the original comic book. In the first *X-Men* there are no Latinos, not even as janitors. In *X-Men 2* (2003) we do glimpse (inside the federal building) a Latino janitor (Alfonso Quijada). In Gavin Hood's *X-Man Origins: Wolverine* (2009) we catch sight of a young Scott Summers learning Spanish from an unnamed Latina teacher (Alison Araya).

The first time a Latinx mutant appears in the X-Men filmic universe is when director Matthew Vaughn introduces the Latina winged mutant Angel Salvadore (also known as Tempest) in *X-Men: First Class* (2011). That she's a character in hiding because of her racialized identity as a mutant is subordinated (completely elided) to Vaughn's presentation of her as a stripper. Whether racialized as mutant or Latina, in Vaughn's film world the results are the same: greater interest in hypersexualizing a brown woman's body than in establishing her interesting origin story that *doesn't* include mention of her as a stripper: escape from an abusive stepfather and transmogrification into a human with insect wings, an ability to crawl on walls and fly, and to digest food like a fly. (See writer Grant Morrison and artist Ethan Van Sciver's *New X-Men*, vol. 1, #118, 2001.)

The X-Men films tend not to overtly mark the Latino mutants as *Latino*. Their Latinoness is erased either by casting actors who pass as white or are white, or whom audiences will read as African American. With *X-Men: First Class* Vaughn and his creative team cast Jewish African American Zoe Kravitz. In this same film, the Latino mutant Janos ("Riptide") appears, but as played by the Spanish actor Alex Gonzalez. So, too, does the Latino mutant Armando Muñoz ("Darwin"), but as played by the Kenyon-born actor, Edi Gathegi.

Figure 97. Zoe Kravitz as Angel Salvadore in Matthew Vaughn's *X-Men: First Class* (2011).

In the comic book film franchise, where one would expect Latinos to appear front and center, they do not. In casting and origin-story modifications, the Latinx supermutants in the in-print comic books are simply erased.

As already mentioned, when Latinos/as are present, they are hypersexualized, criminalized, or re-racialized within a black/ white paradigm. They are also the buffoons. In *Ant-Man* (2015) director Peyton Reed and his creative team cast Michael Peña as Luis, sidekick and comic relief to Anglo Scott Lang's (Paul Rudd) high-tech wizardry. Both are criminals, but Luis is petty thief to Lang's genius, save-the-world technology hacks. After Luis picks Lang up from jail in a beat-up van, he tells Lang how his girlfriend left him, his dad got deported, and his mom died. And while the film's writers Edgar Wright and Joe Cornish do try to complicate the Latino stereotype by writing in to Luis's script lines that show him to have a distinguished taste in high art ("You know me, I'm more of a neo-Cubist kind of guy but there was this one Rothko that was sublime"), in the end, he's still the Latino buffoon and sidekick to the Anglo superhero.

Figure 98. Edi Gathegi as Darwin in *X-Men: First Class*.

In closing, let me mention the casting of Latina Zoe Saldana in comic book films that literally re-create her as an alien Other (Neytiri in James Cameron's *Avatar* or Gamora in James Gunn's *Guardians of the Galaxy*), code 'her as African American, or embrace her Afrolatinidad. Rather than spend time rehashing how Latinoness is made safe as the exotic, eco-friendly alien in *Avatar*, or how she turns from alien warrior to soothing sidekick to bumbling terrestrial Anglo Starlord Peter Quill (Chris Pratt), let me focus on two comic book films made by French directors that begin to move in the right direction, at least in their casting of Saldana and writing of characters for her.

First, there's French director Sylvain White's re-creation of Andy Diggle (writer) and Jock's (artist) *The Losers* (Vertigo, 2013), in which Saldana appears as Aisha, one of several mercenaries that include Jenson (a buff Chris Evans); two African Americans, Pooch (Columbus Short) and Roque (Idris Elba); and another Latino, Cougar (Óscar Jaenada). While the film uses landscapes (Bolivia and Puerto Rico, filled with brown bikinied women) to establish the exoticness of the story in stereotypical ways, we see Saldana as Aisha play against stereotypes. She's arguably the smartest of the bunch, *and* she resists being sexualized. Second, there's *Colombiana* (2011). Not directly re-created from a comic book (DC or Marvel or any other), it does convey an anything-goes comic book sensibility; likely this is due to the presence of Luc Besson (France's comic book filmmaker par excellence) as co-writer and producer. Under Olivier Megaton's direction, Saldana as the character Cataleya is given an origin story firmly anchored in her Afrolatinidad. The film opens in Bogotá, Colombia, and introduces the audience to her and her parents, who are killed (and become the source of the vengeance narrative). Megaton casts the recognizable Latino actor Jesse Borrego as her father, Fabio Restrepo; he casts mixed Ghanian and Anglo actress Cynthia Addai-Robinson as the mother, Alicia.

When her father gives her the cattleya orchid necklace, he shares with her its long history within the family. The film anchors her origin story in family ancestry. In making Saldana into the adult Afrolatina action superhero, she always wears the necklace and never forgets her ancestry. And, while ultimately she seeks revenge on those who murdered her parents, she acquires a powerful political approach to her worldview that is manifest especially in her look: beret and army fatigues. We finally get a Blatina superhero, but one firmly rooted in her ancestry and the black and brown political struggles of our ancestors: the brown and black power movements of the late 1960s and early '70s.

We see with a film like *Colombiana* that it is possible to make filmic superhero storyworlds with complex Latinx superheroes. And, while Megaton doesn't get it all right, even when it begins to slip into a sexualization of Saldana as Cataleya, the film demonstrates a certain critical self-awareness of this stereotype of Latina superheroes. The grand action sequence that follows her battling her enemies while all gunned-up and in her underwear turns into a hand-to-hand fight, where she uses everyday domestic and feminized objects (hair brush and cleaning objects like a toilet plunger) to subdue her enemy, poking fun at those silver screen narratives of Latinas as only passive and domestic. We see here that it is possible to create Latinx superhero characters that embrace their racial, ethnic, and gendered identities in empowering ways.

Figure 99. Cataleya wearing the family heirloom necklace and a Captain America T-shirt in *Colombiana* (2011).

While there are some superhero films, animations, and TV shows that re-create Latinx superheroes and characters in complex ways, most *willfully* erase, assimilate, hypersexualize, and re-racialize Latinos. And this, even though there have been some great strides forward made in the in-print superhero comic book universe. And this, even though in the United States today Latinos

Multimediated Latinx Superheroes

Figure 100. Zoe Saldana as Black Power movement–style Cataleya in Olivier Megaton's *Colombiana* (2011).

are the majority minority population. There's a sense that somehow putting Latinos in front of the screen as the superhero protagonists will diminish audience interest and profits made. The introduction of Latinx superheroes isn't a zero sum marketplace equation. Their more forceful introduction and complex creation in film, animation, and TV would offer innovative modifications of in-print comic book protoworlds. It would be a more accurate distillation and re-creation of our contemporary world, along with the concerns of a richer and more diverse population of readers. In this way, they might, as Aldo Regaldo writes more generally of the need to diversify comics, "challenge comic book audiences to consider the aesthetic, cultural, and historical truths that underpin the genre of superhero fiction and, by extension, the culture at large" (225). And in so doing, we might see the making of more Latinx superhero film, animation, and televisual narratives tomorrow that distill and re-create in wondrously imaginative ways Latinx building blocks that make up in-print comic books and the world today.

UP, UP . . . AND *AWAY!*

In a 2005 interview, Stan Lee considers how there likely exists a comic book that is as "worthwhile as a Shakespearean play" (McLaughlin, *Stan Lee: Conversations*, 188). After imagining a scenario where Shakespeare and Michelangelo team up to create a comic book, he reminds us that good comics can be made; it just depends on "who does it and how it is done" (188). He forcefully reminds us that just as there can be well-made and poorly made comics, so, too, can there be "bad novels, good novels, bad ballets, bad operas, and good ones. Everything depends on the quality, not on the manner in which it is presented" (188). I begin the ending of this book with Lee for two reasons: one, to insist on the fact that comic book storyworlds (print, animated, televisual, and filmic) are worthy of our time and energy; and two, to remind us that some do a good job, and others a sloppy job, including centrally those that choose to distill and reconstruct a reality that includes Latinos/as—and that today is increasingly becoming majority Latinx.

Certainly we've seen some doozies, and across the different storytelling formats: print comics, animation, TV shows, and film. This seems counterintuitive, and not just in terms of the relay race of human creativity that, since time immemorial, has passed the baton from one creator who ups the ante on another creator. It doesn't make business sense. Latinos in the United States represent a $1.8 trillion buying power. We consume. We consume mass culture. We go to the movies the most. We play videogames the most. We watch TV the most. It would make business sense, then, for us to be represented in a mass culture inclusive of comic book storyworlds in all its guises. Yet in the mainstream, corporate-driven creation of superhero comics, animation, TV, and film we are either willfully erased or barely present. Take Marvel's *Runaways* (2003–2015), in which Brian K. Vaughan uses his creative capacity to realize a compelling story about a multicultural superhero band of teens who turn against their evil, murderous supervillain parents—but falls short by not creating any Latinos. And, when Latinos are present, it's often fleetingly. For instance, with DC's launch of its New 52 reboots we saw the birth and rebirth of a handful of A-list superheroes *as* Latino. We also saw their quick disappearance if they didn't hit profit goals increasingly needed to feed DC stockholders' percentage profit minimums. When profits become the name of the game, comic book storyworlds rely on brand loyalty, A-list iconic characters, and bigger and better SFX bangs for the buck. We see the cranking out of multiverse upon multiverse to test-market old characters with new identities. Sometimes these new identities are Latinx, but for the wrong reason: to see if they'll sell more *just* because, and not because they are artful and compelling. What's lost is making rich visually and verbally constructed Latinx characters with complex journeys and dilemmas; in fact, if they're not turning profit, they're usually killed off or canceled. Those comics that do well become teasers for films; and films that do well become teasers for more films of the same kind. Latinx superheroes are one of the victims of this machine that moves lifelessly around and around in its repetition of the same.

As this book has shown, however, we have not rung the final death knell on Latinos in superhero comic book storyworlds. There are some excellent creations out there: the superhero flash animations of Jorge Gutierrez and Adam de la Peña; TV shows like *Heroes Reborn*; those superhero comic book films by Megaton and other directors. There are the many extraordinary creations discussed in chapter 1, including Joe Quesada's Latina superhero Maya Lopez as Echo (*Daredevil*, vol. 2, #9, December 1999) and his superteam of Santerians (*Daredevil*, "Father," #2, October 2005); the multiracial creative alliance whereby Blatino creator Felipe Smith (writer), African American Damion Scott (artist), and Anglo Tradd Moore invent the psychologically complex and kinetically geometrized Robbie Reyes as the new Ghost Rider (*All-New Ghost Rider*); Michael Bendis (writer) and Sara Pichelli's (artist) Brooklyn-born-and-raised teen, Miles Morales as the Ultimate Spider-Man; Scott Lobdell (writer) and Brett Booth's (artist) Miguel José Barragon as Bunker (*Teen Titans*); Keith Giffen's (#1–10), John Rogers's, and Cully Hamner's Jaime Reyes as the new Blue Beetle; Orson Scott Card's Antoñio Stark (*Ultimate Iron Man*, vol. 1), Fred Van Lente (writer) and Pakistani/Austrian/Turkish artist

Mahmud Asrar's Victor Alvarez as Hell's Kitchen's new Power Man (*Shadowland: Power Man* #1, 2010), among others. And there are those like Mike Mignola, who sends his Hellboy character south of the proverbial Tortilla Curtain. In his five-story collection *Hellboy in Mexico* (2016), Mignola, with artist Richard Corben and Latino twins Fábio Moon and Gabriel Bá, infuses a hyperexpressionistic geometrizing Mignola style to character and storyworld that energizes and complicates not only Hellboy but also the Mexican *luchadores* and Mexican mythical figures he encounters. In the writing and geometrizing of story, we see a will to style that evidences a responsibility and respect to Mexican culture. (See also Scott Bukatman, *Hellboy's World: Comics and Monsters on the Margins*, in which he also discusses Mexican director Guillermo del Toro's filmic re-creations of *Hellboy*.) If we see this will to style translate into the making of animation, TV, and film, we will also see superhero narratives that challenge racial stereotypes. Christian Davenport remarked on the trend in comic books to increasingly create African American superheroes with a "greater variety of superpowers; better employment; more articulate characters; a greater balance between acts of brute force, athleticism, and intelligence" (206). Jeffrey A. Brown observes a similar trend in diversity with superheroes more generally, noting how "numerous African-American, female, Asian, Middle-Eastern, Jewish, and queer superheroes headline their own series or are significant members of super teams. If the current film and television expression of the superhero genre continues to follow the lead of comic books there is a huge potential for a world of superheroes that truly reflects American culture" (*The Modern Superhero in Film and Television*, e-book). We're beginning to see this complexity gain traction in television. And with James Mangold's film *Logan* (2017) we're beginning to see it bear out in Marvel Studio films, too. While the film opens with the typical racist representations of Latinos as tattooed cholo gangbangers—a drunken Wolverine skewers them all—over the course of the narrative Mangold reverses age-old stereotypes and white masculinist ideals. Mangold kills off the white male saviors (Wolverine and Professor Xavier) and foregrounds the arrival of a new generation of mutants of color: Latinx tweens born south of the U.S.-Mexico border such as Spanish-speaking Laura, Delilah, and Julio Rictor, as well as African American Bobby. They leave Wolverine six feet under and cross the border into Canada—the new Eden. They are the world's new tribe and promise of a new, racially diverse superhero future.

Like Jeffrey A. Brown, I remain optimistic. I remain so because of all those skillful creations by Latinos working behind the scenes as creators (artists mostly), who have been the life force of mainstream, in-print, and superhero comics generally. They are many (see the appendix). While they remain the unsung heroes, they are the powerful generators of creativity in the DC and Marvel industry.

I remain optimistic also because there are Latinos who bring a great degree of a will to style in their distillation and re-creation of ways that make new our perception, thought, and feeling of Latinx identity and experience. I think readily of the following: Frank Espinosa's *Rocketo*, which breathes new life into the form with his refashioning of German Expressionist art to create a sci-fi, epic-dimensioned storyworld that follows the protagonist, the Mapper Rocketo, a figure distilled and reconstructed from Espinosa's own experience of exile and displacement as a Cuban; John Gonzalez's (*The Elites*) and Andrew Huerta's (*Sovereign*) creation of multi-cultural superhero teams that include fully fleshed-out Latino protagonists; Jules Rivera's Latina-centric sci-fi superhero adventure, *Valkyrie Squadron*; J. Gonzo's use of retro visuals to geometrize the creation of his *luchador* superhero in *La Mano del Destino*; Hector Rodriguez's creation of the monolingual Spanish-speaking, border-dwelling community activist Toro Pesado, in *El Peso Hero*; the creating of contemporary Latino superheroes steeped in ancestrally rich culture and traditions who fight for justice for all, as seen in the comics created by Fernando Rodriguez (*Aztec of the City*), Javier Hernandez (*El Muerto*), Rafael Navarro (Sonambulo), Richard Dominguez (*El Gato Negro*), Alex Olivas (*Tzolkin*), Daniel Parada (*Zotz: Serpent and Shield*), Jaime "Jimmy" Portillo (*Hell Paso*), and Laura Molina (*The Jaguar*); Carlos Saldaña's creating of an anthropomorphic Latino superhero with his serape-wearing, time-traveling Burrito. And there's the complex tapestry of narratives created by Jaime Hernandez that intertwine the tellurian with the galactic to create a radically new superhero aesthetic that collapses mainstream with the margins: superheroes (Stan Lee, Jack Kirby, and Steve Ditko) with cartoon strip (Hank Ketcham's

Dennis the Menace) with everyday life (Dan DeCarlo's *Archie*) with counterculture (R. Crumb and Spain Rodriguez) with punk attitude (Sid Vicious's *Sex Pistols*). For Jaime, there's no reason *not* to include rocket ships and dinosaurs along with everyday life in the Latino barrio. For instance, he invests his Tejana protagonist Penny Century as Beatríz García with a deep love of superhero comics and a desire to perform as a superhero in her everyday life as a Latina. In several of Hernandez's multigenerational Latina-superhero-populated serialized comics (collected and published as *God and Science: Return of the Ti-Girls*, 2012) we're immersed in a world filled with conflicts and battles—and largely absent of men; when there are infants, they're tucked away in belt buckles. In addition to Penny Century we meet superheroes like Espectra (Maggie's pro wrestler cousin, Xochitl Navas, grown old), the Weeper, the robot Cheetah Torpeda from the planet Blotos, and Space Queen.

Figure 101. Jaime Hernandez's *God and Science: Return of the Ti-Girls* (2012).

Shelly Streeby remarks on how Hernandez's foregrounding of aging Latinas functions as "the site of plenitude and the locus of amazing, generative powers rather than a phobic, diminished, sad object" (162). More generally, Matt Yokey sees this as Hernandez's way of subverting "the homogenizing strategies of national rhetoric and of mass culture," the undermining of "an Anglo-American master narrative sustained by the Silver Age superhero comics," and the radical complicating of "the utopian impulse that resides at the heart of the genre" (1). And, with Hernandez, Latina superheroes are not just of the sci-fi variety—and U.S.-inspired. We see with his creation of Rena Titañon, for instance, how the Latina *luchadora* (masked and unmasked) also functions as superhero. Ellen Gil-Gomez identifies Hernandez's creating of Latina *luchadoras* as clearing the narrative space for an "alternative matriarchal family structure" (124). With Hernandez's Latina superheroes, who appear in all different shapes, sizes, generations, and strengths, we see how the superhero can and does have the power to radically expand and make new our engagement with comic book reconstructions of the experiences and identities of Latinos today. (See Aldama, *Latinx Comic Book Storytelling*.)

Today, the vital spirit of these Latinx-created superheroes is permeating those we think of as more mainstream comics. For instance, Edgardo Miranda-Rodríguez introduced the undocumented Joaquín Torres as a new Latino Falcon; after crossing the U.S.-Mexico border at age six, then excelling at school, he's a superhero invested in the community, especially saving other border crossers.

Figure 102. Backstory of Joaqúin Torres in *Captain America: Sam Wilson*, #1 (December 2015).

And in 2016, Miranda-Rodríguez created the New York–born Afrolatina La Borinqueña, who learns of her superpowers (wind and water) after visiting Puerto Rico. The same year, Miranda-Rodríguez also set the *Guardians of Infinity* series in a Latino New York: Groot and Ben Grimm (The Thing) land in New York City's Lower East Side, where they ride buses, meander around Avenue D's Jacob Riis public-housing project, and encounter Latinos shooting hoops and *viejitos* and *viejitas* playing dominoes. And we learn of Groot's Afrolatino roots when an unnamed Latina *viejita* identifies him as a relative of the ceiba tree that grows in the Caribbean and has become a symbol of anticolonial resistance: "I know he's the Ceiba, I can feel the spirits of our ancestors inside him," she tells her grandson, Kian.

Figure 103. Abuelita explains anticolonial significance of the ceiba tree in *Guardians of Infinity* (January 2016).

March 1, 2017, saw the arrival of the LGBTQ celebrated America Chavez (her lesbian mamas and her sexually nuanced witty banter with and desire for Kate Bishop) as the eponymous hero of her own series, *America*. It's written by author of YA lesbian fiction Gabby Rivera, and drawn by Joe Quinones. Gabby Rivera informs readers that Chavez is no longer doing "the Teen Brigade thing" and how she "basically WAS the Young Avengers" but can't go home: her moms have died saving the entire Multiverse. Rivera's narrator ends this expository opening by asking, "So where does a super-strong queer brown girl who can punch star-shaped holes between dimensions go to get her hero-free kicks?" Chavez breaks with her girlfriend, Lisa, attends Sotomayor University, and continues to bust supervillain chops, including white fraternity-boy cyborgs ("The Girls Wanna Be Her," #2). And, there are plans at Image Comics for writer Joe Casey and artist Nick Dragotta to introduce the superhero America Vasquez in *All America Comix*. We see here as elsewhere some of the best comic book storytelling: the willful use of space design, inking, lettering, balloon placement and size, perspective, and geometric shaping in the creating of rich, compelling, and kinetic Latino superhero comic book storyworlds.

So, while there are plenty of mainstream superhero comic book storyworlds that lack a great degree of what I've been calling a will to style, Latinx artists, authors, and directors *are* creating wonderfully exciting, enriching, and engaging in-print superhero comics. And this leads me to another reason that I remain optimistic. These Latinx creators *do* encounter the poorly made Latinx superhero comics in all their guises. However, what we see *in action* is that they actively metabolize and make new all that they come across. This is to say that their minds/brains actively transform all those cultural objects that make up our world, including superhero comic book storyworlds in print, animation, TV, and film formats. Their imagination isn't a blank slate to be etched upon indelibly. Indeed, it is the opposite. They are constantly exercising a variety of mental processes to imagine new possible ways of existing in the world in the present and the future.

There have been many a poorly constructed Latinx superhero figure in mainstream media. However, while they have a certain fixed function (in comics they appear as drawn and fixed within panels, for instance), once caught up in our imagination we transform them into anything and everything. This is also why, when we had few Latino superheroes in DC and Marvel comics, many of us growing up would simply imagine ourselves as a Batman or Superman or some hybrid of the two, as I did. As this book demonstrates, Latinx authors, artists, and directors are extraordinarily creative and *re-creative* in what they do to actively add to and transform mainstream superhero comic book storyworlds—and much more.

This doesn't excuse those who continue to churn out lazy and careless Latinx superheroes. This doesn't let off the hook those who actively erase our presence within these storyworlds. They are accountable—as creators. And we have every right to judge their works as poor products of the imagination and artful production. And, here let me make loud and clear that it is not diversity in comics that we are judging, but how this diversity is re-created. Indeed, of late there has been a backlash against diversity in comics in simpleminded and simplistic terms. For instance, in an interview with Milton Griepp with the online comics trade magazine *ICV2* (*Internal Correspondence Version 2*), David Gabriel, Marvel's VP of sales, stated how readers "didn't want any more diversity" and that they were "turning their nose" at the introduction of diverse characters who were not a "core Marvel character" ("In October, Everything Changed," March 31, 2017). Gabriel came to these conclusions by measuring a drop in sales of issues that featured diverse superheroes. He didn't consider that readers might not be interested in poorly written and poorly geometrized storyworlds that feature diverse superheroes. Moreover, as George Gene Gustines corrects, those that are done well, such as G. Willow Wilson (writer) and Adrian Alphona's (artist) *Ms. Marvel*, which features the Muslim teen Kamala Khan as its superhero, consistently sell in high numbers in digital as well as in-print issues and collected editions; the collected edition *Ms. Marvel: Super Famous* was nominated for the sci-fi and fantasy Hugo Award. Gustines ends his article with a quote from G. Willow Wilson: "Let's scrap the word diversity entirely and replace it with authenticity and realism [. . .] This is not a new world. This is the world" (*New York Times*, April 2, 2017).

I remain optimistic because of the Latinx superhero comic book storyworld creations that turn my everyday life into an art: that make me feel my life is less boring, less repetitive, less monotonous; that satisfy my hunger for experiencing my life and the lives of others in new ways.

No matter the storytelling format, those Latinx superhero comic book storyworlds created with a high degree of a will to style both in content and form take me by the hand and guide me into a labyrinthine world of novelty, where with every step their artful reconstructions show me something new about what it means to be Latinx within the order of the labyrinth. I remain optimistic because the great creators of Latinx superhero comic book storyworlds educate anew my senses. They make me an active and attentive co-creator. They allow me to soar up, up . . . and away!

LOOKING AT THE MAINSTREAM FROM THE INDEPENDENT TRENCHES

An Afterword

As an independent comic book creator who cofounded (and serves as creative director for) the Latino Comics Expo, my main focus is to promote independently produced Latino content by Latino creators. When Frederick Aldama (known as "El Profe" in the Latino comics world) asked me to write the afterword, I hesitated. As one of many DIY Latino comic book creators producing our own Latino-inspired characters, I'd rather keep the spotlight turned away from the corporate media machine's churning out ethnic-flavor-of-the month characters to try to grab our dollars. Then I read *Latinx Superheroes in Mainstream Comic Books* . . .

I'm glad I did. This well-researched book cracks open the catacombs of yesteryear's mainstream comics, shining a bright light on the significant presence (some better than others) of Latino superheroes who have shaped this history. Reading *Latinx Superheroes* reminded me that my first exposure to Latino characters was in that mass media universe El Profe refers to as "storyworlds." I don't remember the media itself (in-print comic, film, or TV show) when I first discovered Zorro, but I do recall imagining a character dressed in a fanciful black costume, riding atop a horse while brandishing swords and a gun. No matter his Spanish origin, I imagined myself, a Latino kid with Mexican ancestry, as this superhero. I do remember clearly the first time I read in-print comics featuring Marvel's Puerto Rican martial arts superhero, Hector Ayala as White Tiger. First in a two-issue story arc in *Peter Parker: The Spectacular Spider-Man*, a year later in *The Human Fly*, and then his sporadic appearances in various Marvel titles. This was the first time I could look at a comic book and see a Spanglish-speaking superhero. My eleven-year-old ethnic sensibilities didn't pick up the subtle differences in his Latinoness—that he's Puerto Rican and not Mexican—and this didn't matter. To me, he was a superhero who spoke Spanglish and had a Mexican-sounding name. He was a superhero I could completely relate to.

As El Profe illustrates in this book, it's really through the mainstream *mass* media that Latinos (and all others) become aware of all that makes up our world. Picking those White Tiger comics off the spinner rack at my local 7-Eleven allowed me to enjoy the latest exploits of Spider-Man and the Human Fly. And, White Tiger demonstrated how superheroes could also come from the same household that I grew up in. A comic book superhero didn't have to be raised by a silver-haired white couple. He or she could come from a Spanish-speaking Latino home like I did. Bill Mantlo and George Pérez didn't just introduce another martial arts character in *Deadly Hands of Kung-Fu* #19, they karate chopped a hole in the wall of the Marvel universe for us Latinos to see ourselves and breathe anew. Dragon

In between my trips to the 7-Eleven and moments of imagining myself as White Tiger along with a panoply of other superheroes, mainstream media was hitting me with all sorts of Latino characters: from Ricky Ricardo (*I Love Lucy*) and Freddy Prinze's young protagonist Chico Rodriguez (*Chico & the Man*) to Speedy Gonzalez and Gomez Addams, among others. Back then the writers and studios weren't concerned with giving depth and complexity to the *actual* richness of our Latino identities and experience. They certainly weren't interested in creating superheroic role models as seen with White Tiger and others that El Profe identifies herein. The captains of the industry were hell-bent on creating Latinos as stereotypical over-sexed buffoons. As El Profe digs up from the past and present archive of Latino superheroes in mainstream comic book storyworlds, some creative teams have gotten it right, and others have slipped into a lazy, careless modus operandi that flattens the Latino experience.

Slowly, U.S. mainstream media creations are reflecting the demographic shifts of our nation. We as Latinos make up 18 percent of the population. It is definitely moving forward with *willfully* constructed (to use El Profe's concept), vital Latino superheroes. While we certainly do need more Latinos working on mainstream creative teams—and with license to actually make compelling characters—we see today so many examples of non-Latino creators bringing their expert drawing and writing skills to bear on the creating of some of the most compelling Latino superheroes, such as Miles Morales as Spider-Man and Robbie Reyes as the new Ghost

Rider. What's indisputable is that the mainstream media will continue to give us Latino superheroes. Done right, they will inspire and empower young Latino readers. When created with a lack of *willfulness*, as stereotypes, or as the token shade of brown to seemingly check off the quota box, Latino readers of comics will shut them out. We will seek other more vital creations. We will continue to make our own, infusing them with all that we love about this written and drawn storytelling medium (the geometrizing of the story, as per El Profe) along with the richness of our Latino culture and experiences.

We Latinos read and view superhero comic book storyworlds in all variety of mainstream media. And, when it's not there, we don't just sit back and ponder the gloom and doom of the industry. We create our own *Latinx* superheroes at once inspired by those great mainstream comic books we all grew up with *and* that push the boundaries even more. Like White Tiger of yesteryear, we're more than ready to rise to this superheroic challenge.

—*Javier Hernandez,*
Creator of El Muerto,
Maniac Priest, and Les
Vodouisants and Co-
founder of the Latino
Comics Expo

APPENDIX

Select Creators of Mainstream Comics

*I include under "artist" those who pencil, ink, and color.

Select Creators of Latinos/as of the Americas

Aguirre, Claudia. Artist.
Albuquerque, Rafael. Artist.
Alcatena, Enrique. Artist. (Argentina)
Alonso, Axel. Editor.
Badilla, Carlos. Artist. (Chile)
Baltazar, Art. Writer and artist.
Benitez, Joe. Writer and artist.
Cabrera, Eva. Artist.
Candelar Harry. Artist.
Cariello, Sergio. Artist.
Collazo, Hector. Artist.
Colon, Ernie. Artist. (Puerto Rico)
Corona, Jorge. Artist.
de la Rosa, Sam. Artist.
Delgado, Edgar. Artist.
Deodato, Mike. Artist. (Brazil)
Doe, Juan. Artist.
Esposito, Taylor. Artist.
Esquivel, Eric M. Writer.
Estrada, Ric. Artist. (Cuba)
Fernandez, Raul. Artist.
Fernández Dávila, Sergio. Artist.
Garcia, Manuel. Artist.
Garcia, Marte. Artist.
García-López, José Luis. Artist.
Garza, Alé. Artist.
Guara Barros, Ig. Artist.
Guinaldo, Andrés. Artist.
Haghenbeck, Francisco. Writer.

Hernandez, Gilbert. Writer and artist.

Huerta, Andrew. Writer and artist.

Jemas, Bill. Writer and editor.

Jiménez, Jorge. Artist.

Jimenez, Phil. Writer and artist.

Marquez, David: Artist.

Martinez, Alitha E. Artist.

Martinez, Kenny. Artist.

Martinez, Roy Allan. Artist.

Medina, Angel. Artist.

Mendoza, Jaime. Artist.

Miranda-Rodríguez, Edgardo. Writer and artist.

Molinar, Larry. Artist.

Morales, Mark. Artist.

Morales, Ralph. Artist.

Moreira, Rubèn. Writer and artist. (Puerto Rico)

Moreno, Chris. Artist.

Navarro, Rafael. Writer and artist.

Neves, Fabiano. Artist. (Brazil)

Nicienza, Fabian. Writer and editor.

Olazaba, Victor. Artist. (Brazil)

Pansica, Eduardo. Artist

Passalaqua, Allen. Artist.

Pérez, George. Writer and artist.

Pérez, Ramón K. Artist.

Pinna, Amilcar. Artist. (Brazil)

Pinto, Oscar. Writer.

Plascencia, FCO. Artist. (Mexico)

Prado, Joe. Artist.

Quesada, Joe. Writer, artist, editor.

Quinones, Joe. Artist.

Quintana, Wil. Artist.

Ramos, Wilson, Jr. Artist.

Ramos, Humberto. Artist.

Ramos, Rodney. Artist.

Rio, Alvaro. Artist.

Rodriguez, Anibal. Artist.

Rodriguez, Dan. Artist.

Rodriguez, Tone (Antonio). Artist.

Rosado, Rafael. Artist.
Rosado, William. Artist.
Saltares, Javier. Artist.
Sanchez, Alex. Artist.
Sanchez Madrigal, Carlos Benjamin. Artist. (Mexico)
Santacruz, Derlis. Writer and artist. (Argentina)
Santolouco, Mateus. Artist. (Brazil)
Schomburg, Alex (Alejandro Schomburg y Rosa). Artist.
Serra, Gabriel. Artist. (Uruguay)
Serrano, Felix. Artist.
Silva, Adriano. Artist.
Smith, Felipe. Writer and artist.
Sotomayor, Chris. Artist.
Texeira, Mark. Artist.
Timms, John. Artist. (Costa Rica)
Vazquez, Gustavo. Artist. (Puerto Rico)
Velez, Ivan, Jr. Writer.

Select Creators of Latinos/as of Asia (Filipinos)

Alcala, Alfredo. Artist.
"Chua" Chan, Ernie. Artist.
DeZuniga, Tony. Artist.
Gan, Steve. Artist.
Niño, Alex. Artist.
Portacio, Whilce. Writer and artist.
Redondo, Nester. Artist.

WORKS CITED

Theory

Aldama, Frederick Luis. *Your Brain on Latino Comics: From Gus Arriola to Los Bros Hernandez*. Austin: University of Texas Press, 2009.

——. "Getting Your Mind/Body On." In *Latinos and Narrative Media: Participation and Portrayal*, edited by Frederick Luis Aldama, 241–58. New York: Palgrave Macmillan, 2013.

——. *Latinx Comic Book Storytelling: An Odyssey by Interview*. San Diego State University Press, 2016.

Baetens, Jan. "Abstractions in Comics." *SubStance* 40, no. 1 (2011): 94–113.

Betancourt, David. "'All-New Ghost Rider': Creative Muscle to the Reborn Spirit of Vengeance," *Washington Post*, October 14, 2014. Web. Accessed November 30, 2016. https://www.washingtonpost .com/news/comic-riffs/wp/2014/10/14/all-new-ghost-rider -felipe-smith-brings-creative-muscle-to-the-reborn-spirit-of -vengeance/.

Bieloch, Katharina, and Sharif Bitar. "Batman Goes Transnational: The Global Appropriation and Distribution of an American Hero." In *Transnational Perspectives on Global Narratives: Comics at the Crossroads*, edited by Shane Denson, Christina Meyer, and Daniel Stein, 113–26. London, New York: Bloomsbury Academic, 2013.

Bukatman, Scott. *Hellboy's World: Comics and Monsters on the Margins*. Berkeley: University of California Press, 2016.

Burke, Liam. *The Comic Book Film Adaptation*. Jackson: University Press of Mississippi, 2015.

Cleger, Osvaldo. "Why Video Games: Ludology Meets Latino Studies." In *The Routledge Companion to Latina/o Popular Culture*, edited by Frederick Luis Aldama, 87–100. New York: Routledge, 2016.

Coogan, Peter. *Superhero: The Secret Origin of a Genre*. Austin, Tex.: Monkeybrain Books, 2006.

Davenport, Christian. "Black Is the Color of My Comic Book Character: An Examination of Ethnic Stereotypes." In *Drawing the Line: Comics Studies and Inks, 1994–1997*, edited by Lucy Shelton

Caswell and Jared Gardner, 196–209. Columbus: The Ohio State University Press, 2017.

Denison, Rayna, and Rachel Mizsei-Ward, eds. *Superheroes on World Screens*. Jackson: University Press of Mississippi, 2015.

Dittmer, Jason. *Captain America and the Nationalist Superhero: Metaphors, Narratives, and Geopolitics*. Philadelphia: Temple University Press, 2013.

Ellis, Mark, and Melissa Martin Ellis. *The Everything Guide to Writing Graphic Novels*. Avon, Mass.: Adams Media, 2008.

Espinoza, Mauricio. "The Alien Is Here to Stay." In *Graphic Borders: Latino Comic Books Past, Present, and Future*, edited by Frederick Luis Aldama and Christopher González, 181–202. Austin: University of Texas Press, 2016.

Fawaz, Ramzi. *The New Mutants: Superheroes and the Radical Imagination of American Comics*. New York: NYU Press, 2016.

Frank, Kathryn. "Everybody Wants to Rule the Multiverse: Latino Spider-Men in Marvel's Media Empire." In *Graphic Borders: Latino Comic Books Past, Present, and Future*, edited by Frederick Luis Aldama and Christopher González, 241–51. Austin: University of Texas Press, 2016.

Gardner, Jared. "Storylines." *SubStance* 40, no. 1 (2011): 53–69.

Gil-Gómez, Ellen. "Wrestling with Comic Genres and Genders: Luchadores as Signifiers in Sonambulo and Locas." In *Graphic Borders: Latino Comic Books Past, Present, and Future*, edited by Frederick Luis Aldama and Christopher González, 109–29. Austin: University of Texas Press, 2016.

Gray, Richard J., and Betty Kaklimanidou. *The 21st Century Superhero: Essays on Gender, Genre, and Globalization in Film*. Jefferson, N.C.: McFarland, 2011.

Griepp, Milton. "In October, Everything Changed." March 31, 2017, https://icv2.com/articles/news/view/37152/marvels-david -gabriel-2016-market-shift.

Gustines, George Gene. "Don't Blame These Heroes for Slumping Sales." *New York Times*, April 2, 2017.

Hatfield, Charles. *Hands of Fire: The Comics Art of Jack Kirby*. Jackson: University Press of Mississippi, 2011.

History Channel. "Comic Book Superheroes Unmasked." Posted on May 26, 2013. https://www.youtube.com/watch?v=Ygx_rUJ3XaI.

Hutcheon, Linda. *Theory of Adaptation*. New York: Routledge, 2006.

Johnson, Derek. "Wolverine: Marvel's Mutation from Monthlies to Movies." In *Film and Comic Books*, edited by Ian Gordon, Mark Jancovich, and Matthew P. MacAllister, 64–85. Jackson: University of Mississippi Press, 2007.

Kukonnen, Karin. "Comics as a Test Case for Transmedial Narratology." *SubStance* 40, no. 1 (2011): 34–52.

Lawrence, Christopher. *Storyteller: Three Decades of George Pérez*. Runnemeade, N.J.: Dynamic Forces, 2006.

Lee, Stan. *How to Draw Comics: From the Legendary Creator of Spider-Man, The Incredible Hulk, Fantastic Four, X-Men, and Iron Man*. Watson-Guptill, 2010.

———. *How to Write Comics: From the Legendary Creator of Spider-Man, The Incredible Hulk, Fantastic Four, X-Men, and Iron Man*. New York: Watson-Guptill, 2011.

Lefèvre, Pascal. "Some Medium-Specific Qualities of Graphic Sequences." *SubStance* 40, no. 1 (2011): 14–33.

Marco, Arnaudo. *The Myth of the Superhero*. Translated by Jamie Richards. Baltimore: Johns Hopkins University Press, 2013.

McEniry, Matthew, Robert Moses Peaslee, and Robert G. Weiner. *Marvel Comics into Film: Essays on Adaptations Since the 1940s*. Jefferson, N.C.: McFarland, 2016.

McLaughlin, Jeff, ed. *Stan Lee Conversations*. Jackson: University of Mississippi Press, 2007.

McHale, Brian. "Things Then Did Not Delay in Turning Curious": Some Version of Alice 1966–2010." Web. Accessed November 20, 2016. https://projectnarrative.osu.edu/about/current-research/lectures-and-presentations/mchale.

Nama, Adilifu, and Maya Hadad "Mapping the *Blatino* Badlands and Borderlands of American Pop Culture." In *Graphic Borders: Latino Comic Books Past, Present, and Future*, edited by Frederick Luis Aldama and Christopher González, 252–68. Austin: University of Texas Press, 2016.

Negrón-Muntaner, Frances. "The Latino Media Gap: the State of Latinos in U.S. Media." Web. Accessed December 23, 2016. https://www.youtube.com/watch?v=U6PC0gix1Yk.

Packard, Stephan. "Closing the Open Signification: Forms of Transmedial Storyworlds and Chronotopoi in Comics." *Storyworlds: A Journal of Narrative Studies* 7, no. 2 (Winter 2015): 55–74.

PBS. "Superheroes: A Never-Ending Battle." October 15, 2013. http://www.pbs.org/superheroes/home/.

Penix-Tadson, Phillip. *Cultural Code: Video Games and Latin America*. Cambridge, Mass.: MIT Press, 2016.

Pérez, George. *Focus on George Pérez*. Seattle: Fantagraphic Books, 1985.

Place-Verghnes, Floriane. *Tex Avery: A Unique Legacy*. Bloomington: Indiana University Press, 2006.

Pratt, Henry John. "Making Comics into Film." In *The Art of Comics: A Philosophical Approach*, edited by Aaron Meskin and Roy T. Cook, 147–64. Hoboken, N.J.: Wiley-Blackwell, 2012.

Regalado, Aldo J. *Bending Steel: Modernity and the American Superhero*. Jackson: University of Mississippi Press, 2015.

Risner, Jonathan. "'Authentic' Latinas/os and Queer Characters in Alternative and Mainstream Comics." In *Multicultural Comics: From Zap to Blue Beetle*, edited by Frederick Luis Aldama, 39–54. Austin: University of Texas Press, 2010.

Rodríguez, Richard. T. "Revealing Secret Identities." In *Graphic Borders: Latino Comic Books Past, Present, and Future*, edited by Frederick Luis Aldama and Christopher González, 224–37. Austin: University of Texas Press, 2016.

Rohr, Monica. "Caped Crusaders with Latino Flair." *Hispanic Living*, Fall 2016: 16–17.

Ryan, Marie-Laure. "Transmedial Storytelling and Transfictionality." *Poetics Today* 34, no. 3 (Fall 2013): 361–88.

Sanderson, Peter, Tom DeFalco, Tom Brevoort, and Andrew Darling. *Marvel Encyclopedia: The Definitive Guide to the Characters of the Marvel Universe, s.v. "The Punisher."* New York: DK, 2006.

Serrato, Philip. "Postmodern Guacamole: Lifting the Lid on *El Tigre: The Adventures of Manny River.*" In *Latino Latinos and Narrative Media: Participation and Portrayal*, edited by Frederick Luis Aldama, 71–84. New York: Palgrave Macmillan, 2014.

Streeby, Shelley. "Reading Jaime Hernandez's Comics as Speculative Fiction." *Aztlán: A Journal of Chicano Studies* 40, no. 2 (Fall 2015): 147–66.

Thon, Jan-Noël. *Transmedial Narratology and Contemporary Media Culture*. Lincoln: University of Nebraska Press, 2016.

Wartenberg, Thomas E. "Wordy Pictures: Theorizing the Relationship Between Image and Text in Comics." In *The Art of Comics: A Philosophical Approach*, 87–104. Hoboken, N.J.: Wiley-Blackwell, 2012.

Wells, Paul. *Animation: Genre and Authorship*. London and New York: Wallflower, 2002.

Yockey, Matt. "Ti-Girl Power: American Utopianism in the Queer Superhero Text." *European Journal of American Studies* 10, no. 2 (Summer 2015): 1–16.

Comic Books

Augustyn, Brian (writer), and Sal Velluto (artist). *Firebrand*, #1. New York: DC, February 1996.

———. *Firebrand*, #2. "Burning Bright." New York: DC, March 1996.

———. *Firebrand*, #3. "The Best of Families." New York: DC, April 1996.

———. *Firebrand*, #5. "Killer's Garden." New York: DC, June 1996.

———. *Firebrand*, #6. "Saints and Sinners." New York: DC, July 1996.

———. *Firebrand*, #7. "Opie and His Pals." New York: DC, August 1996.

———. *Firebrand*, #7. "Teach Your Children." New York: DC, August 1996.

———. *Firebrand*, #9. "Final Notice." New York: DC, October 1996.

Avery, Fiona (writer), and Mark Brooks (artist). *Araña: The Heart of the Spider, Vol. 1*. New York: Marvel, March 2005.

Beck, C. C. *Captain Marvel Adventures, #35*. "Radar, the International Policeman." New York: Marvel, May 1944.

Bendis, Brian Michael, Stefano Caselli, and Marte Garcia. *Invincible Iron Man: Ironheart, Vol. 1*. New York: Marvel, 2017.

———. *Invincible Iron Man, #10*. New York: Marvel, May 2016.

Bendis, Michael (writer), and David Marquez (artist). *Miles Morales: The Ultimate Spider-Man, Vol. 2: Revelations*. New York: Marvel, June 2015.

Bendis, Michael (writer), and Sara Pichelli (artist). *Ultimate Fallout*, #4. "Spider-Man No More." New York: Marvel, August 2011.

Bridwell, Nelson E. (writer) and Alex Saviuk (artist). *DC Comics Presents*, #46. New York: DC, June 1982.

Bridwell, Nelson E. (writer), and Ramona Fradon (artist). *The Super Friends*, vol. 1, #8. "The Mind Killers." New York: DC, November 1977.

Busiek, Kurk, Fabian Nicienza (writers), and Scott McDaniel (artist). *Trinity*, #3. "Earth to Rita." New York: DC, 2008.

Busiek, Kurt (writer), and Brent Anderson (artist). *Astro City*, #13. Berkeley: Image Comics, February 1998.

Card, Orson Scott (writer), Andy Kubert, and Mark Bagley (artists). *Ultimate Iron Man, Vol. 1., #1–5*. New York: Marvel, October 2006.

Carlin, Mike (writer), Jerry Ordway, Klaus Janson, and Art Adams (artists). *Secret Origins of Justice League, #33*. "Escapism." New York: DC, December 1988.

Casey, Joe (writer), and Nick Dragotta (artist). *Vengeance, #1*. New York: Marvel, July 2011.

Choi, Brandon (writer), and J. Scott Campbell (artist). *Gen¹³, vol. 2, #7*. New York: Wildstorm/DC, 1995.

Claremont, Chris (writer), and Sal Buscema (artist). *New Mutants, #8*. "The Road to . . . Rome." New York: Marvel, October 1983.

Claremont, Chris (writer), and Bob McLeod (artist). *Marvel Graphic Novel, Vol. 1: The New Mutants, #4*. New York: Marvel, September 1982.

Conway, Gerry (writer), and Chuck Patton (artist). *Justice League of America, vol. 1, #233*. "Rebirth One." New York: DC, December 1984.

Conway, Gerry (writer), and Don Newton (artist). *Detective Comics, vol. 1, #511*. "The 'I' of the Beholder." New York: DC, February 1982. Print.

David, Peter (writer), and Rick Leonardi (artist). *The Amazing Spider-Man, #365*. New York: Marvel, August 1992.

Diggle, Andy (writer), and Jock (artist). *The Losers: Book One*. New York: Vertigo, 2010.

Dixon, Chuck (writer), Rodolfo Damaggio, and Robert Campanella (artists). *Green Arrow, vol. 2, #111*. "Hard Traveling Heroes." New York: DC, August 1996.

Dixon, Chuck (writer), Beau Smith, and Sergio Cariello (artists). *Batman/Wildcat, vol. 1, #1*. "The Pay-Per-Pain Event of the Year." New York: DC, April 1997.

Dixon, Chuck (writer), and Enrique Alcatena (artist). *Flash Annual, vol. 2, #13*. New York: DC, September 2000.

Dixon, Chuck, Doug Moench (writers), and Graham Nolan (artist). *Batman: Knightfall, Vol. 1*. New York: DC, 1993–1994.

Dominguez, Richard. *El Gato Negro, #1–4*. Dallas: Azteca Productions, 1993–1996.

Ellis, Warren (writer), and Bryan Hitch (artist). *Authority, #1*. New York: Wildstorm/DC, May 1999.

Englehart, Steve (writer), and Joe Staton (artist). *Millennium, #1*. New York: DC, January 1988.

Fahey, Kevin, Zach Craley (writers), and Rubine (artist). *Heroes: Vengeance.* "El Vengador." New York: Titan Comics, 2016.

Finger, Bill, David V. Reed (writers), Ira Schnapp, and Charles Paris (artists). *Batman*, #56. "Ride, Bat-Hombre, Ride." New York: DC, December 1949.

Fleisher, Michael (writer), and Ernie Chan (artist). *Jonah Hex*, #9. "Carlota Conspiracy." New York: DC, February 1978.

Fox, Gardner (writer), and Harry Lampert (artist). *Flash Comics*, vol. 1, #1. New York: DC, January 1940.

Giffen, Keith, J. M. DeMatteis (writers), Kevin Maguire, and Joe Rubinstein (artists). *Formerly Known as the Justice League*, vol. 1, #1. "A[nother] New Beginning." New York: DC, September 2003.

Gillen, Kieron (writer), and Jaime McKelvie (artist). *Young Avengers*, #1. New York: Marvel, January 2013.

Glass, Adam (writer), and Federico Dalloccohio (artist). *New 52 Suicide Squad*, vol. 4, #1. New York: DC, November 2011.

Gonzalez, Jason "J. Gonzo." *La Mano del Destino*, #1–3. Mesa, Ariz.: Castle & Key Publications, 2011–2013.

Gonzalez, John (writer), Carlos Gonzalez, and Julian Aguilera (artists). *The Elites*. Dream Destinations, 2014.

Goodwin, Archie (writer), and John Byrne (artist). *Wolverine*, vol. 2, #19. "Heroes & Villains." New York: Marvel, December 1989.

Goodwin, Archie (writer), John Romita Sr., and George Tuska (artists). *Luke Cage, Hero for Hire*, #1. New York: Marvel, June 1972.

Grant, Alan (writer), and Norm Brayfogle (artist). *Batman*, vol. 1, #475. New York: DC, March 1992.

Gruenwald, Mark (writer), Paul Near, and Dennis Janke (artists). *Captain America*, #308. "Armadillo!" New York: Marvel, August 1985.

Gruenwald, Mark, David Wohl (writers), M. C. Wyman, and Charles Barnett (artists). *Captain America Annual*, vol. 1, #12. "Blood of Fighter." New York: Marvel, May 1993.

Hamilton, Edmond (writer), and Sheldon Moldoff (artist). *Detective Comics*, #215. New York: DC, January 1955.

Heinberg, Allan (writer), and Jim Cheung (artist). *Young Avengers*, #1. New York: Marvel, February 2005.

Hernandez, Javier. *El Muerto: The Aztec Zombie*, #1. Whittier: Los Comex, 1998.

Huerta, Andrew. *Sovereign*. Web. July 26, 2016. https://www.patreon.com/andrewhuerta.

Iger, M. (author), and Reed Crandall (artist). *Police Comics*, #1. New York: Quality Comics, August 1941.

Jimenez, Phil, Jeff Jensen (writers), and Phil Jimenez (artist). *Team Titans*, #18. "You Can't Go Home Again, Part Two." New York: DC, March 1994.

Jimenez, Phil, Jeff Jensen (writers), and Phil Jimenez (artist). *Team Titans*, #13. "Times Are Far Between (And Few at That)." New York: DC, October 1993.

Johns, Geoff (writer), and David Finch (artist). *Justice League of America*, vol. 3, #2. New York: DC, May 2013.

Johns, Geoff (writer), and George Pérez (artist). *Infinite Crisis*, vol. 1, #4. "Homecoming." New York: DC, March 2006.

Johns, Geoff (writer), Ivan Reis, and Tony S. Daniel (artists). *New 52 Justice League of America*, vol. 3. New York: DC, 2014. Print.

Johns, Geoff (writer), and Ralph "Rags" Morales (artist). *JSA: Black Reign, Vol. 8*. New York: DC, 2005.

———. *JSA*, vol. 2. New York: DC, 2001.

Jones, Gerard (writer), and Mike Parobeck (artist). *El Diablo*, vol. 2, #1. New York: DC, August 1989.

Kanigher, Robert (writer), and Werner Roth (artist). *Superman's Girl Friend Lois Lane*, vol. 1, #110. "Indian Death Charge." New York: DC, May 1971.

Kelly, Joe (writer), Doug Mahnke, and Tom Nguyen (artists). *Justice League of America*, vol. 1, #100. New York: DC, August 2004.

Kelly, Joe (writer), Doug Mahnke, and Lee Bermejo (artists). *Action Comics*, #775. "What's So Funny About Truth, Justice & the American Way?" New York: DC, March 2001.

Kesel, Karl (writer), and Steve Mattsson (artist). *Superboy and the Ravers*, #1. New York: DC, September 1996.

Kreisberg, Andrew (writer), and Pete Woods (artist). *Justice League of America: Vibe*, vol. 1, #1. "The Breach." New York: DC, February 2013.

Kupperberg, Paul (writer), and Dan Rodriguez (artist). *Justice League Quarterly*, #17. "The Heart of Darkness." New York: DC, December 1994.

Lobdell, Scott (writer), and Carlos Pacheco (artist). *X-Men*, vol. 2, #65. "First Blood." New York: Marvel, June 1997.

Lobdell, Scott (writer) and Brett Booth (artist). *Teen Titans, Vol. 5: The Trial of Kid Flash*. New York: DC, 2015.

———. *Teen Titans*, vol. 4, #3. New York: DC, January 2012.

Mantlo, Bill (writer), and Sal Buscema (artist). *The Incredible Hulk*, vol. 1, #265. New York: Marvel, November 1981.

Mantlo, Bill (writer), and George Pérez (artist). *Deadly Hands of Kung Fu*, #19. New York: Marvel, December 1975.

Mignola, Mike (writer), Richard Corben, Mick Mahoney, Gabriel Bá, and Fábio Moon (artists). *Hellboy in Mexico*. Milwaukie, Ore.: Dark Horse Comics, 2016.

Miligan, Peter (writer), and Mike Allred (artist). *X-Static*, #9. New York: Marvel, April 2003.

Miranda-Rodríguez, Edgardo, and DMC. *Guardians of Infinity*. Web. July 27, 2016. http://www.comicbookresources.com/prev _img.php?pid=64575&disp=ilib&oty=1&oid=72120.

———. *Captain America: Sam Wilson*, #1. New York: Marvel, October 2015.

———. *La Borinqueña*. Web. July 27, 2016. https://www.facebook .com/LaBorinquenaComics.

Molina, Laura. *Cihualyaomiquiz, The Jaguar*. Los Angeles: Laura Molina, 1996.

Morrison, Grant (writer), and Ethan Van Sciver (artist). *New X-Men*, vol. 1, #118. New York: Marvel, November 2001.

Morrison, Grant (writer), and Mark Millar (artist). *Aztek, The Ultimate Man*, #1. New York: DC, August 1996.

Morrison, Grant (writer), Yanick Paquette, and Pere Pérez (artists). *Batman Incorporated*. New York: DC, 2013.

Navarro, Rafael. *Sonambulo: Sleep of the Just*. Los Angeles: Ninth Circle, 1996.

Nitz, Jai (writer), Phil Hester, and Ande Parks (artists). *El Diablo*, vol. 3, #1. New York: DC, November 2008.

Olivas, Alex (writer), and Nick Sirotich (artist). *Tzolkin: Kwotemoks Last Stand*. Washington, D.C.: Tzolkin Comics, 2009.

Parada, Daniel, and Jorge Parada. *Zotz: Serpent and Shield*, #1–2, 2011.

Pfeifer, Will (writer), and Patrick Gleason (artist). *Aquaman*, vol. 6, #16. New York: DC, May 2006.

Pinto, Oscar (writer), Giovanni Barberi, and F. G. Haghenbeck (artists). *Superman Annual*, vol. 2, #12. New York: DC, August 2000.

Portillo, Jaime "Jimmy" (writer), Arturo Delgado, and Ricky Martinez (artists). *Hell Paso: The Story of Dallas Stoudenmire*. Jimmy Daze Comics, 2013.

Priest, Christopher (writer), and Joe Bennett (artist). *The Crew*. New York: Marvel, July 2003–January 2004.

Quesada, Joe (artist), and David Mack (writer). *Daredevil, #2.* "Father." New York: Marvel, October 2005.

———. *Daredevil*, vol. 2, #9. "Murdoch's Law." New York: Marvel, December 1999.

———. *Daredevil, Vol. 2: Parts of a Hole.* New York: Marvel, 2003.

———. *Daredevil: Vision Quest.* New York: Marvel, 2015.

Rivera, Jules. *Valkyrie Squadron.* Web. June 1, 2016. http://www.valkyriesquadron.com.

Rodriguez, Fernando. *Aztec of the City,* #1–4. San Jose, Calif.: El Salto Comics, 1995–1996.

Rodriguez, Hector. *El Peso Hero.* Web. May 3, 2015. http://www.elpesohero.com.

Rucka, Greg, Ed Brubaker (writers), and Michael Lark (artist). *Gotham Central.* New York: DC, 2003.

Saldaña, Carlos. *Burrito, Vol. 1: Burrito Battles the Charming Devil.* Los Angeles: CreateSpace Independent Publishing Platform, 2014.

Simon, Joe (writer), and Jack Kirby (artist). *Star-Spangled Comics,* vol. 1, #7. New York: All-American Publications, April 1942.

Slott, Dan (writer), and Paul Pelletier (artist). *Great Lakes Avengers,* vol. 1, #2. "Dismembership Drive." New York: Marvel, July 2005.

Smith, Felipe (writer), Damion Scott, and Tradd Moore (artists). *All-New Ghost Rider.* Earth-616 series. New York: Marvel, 2014.

Thomas, Dann, Roy Thomas (writers), and Paul Ryan (artist). *Avengers West Coast,* #63. New York: Marvel, October 1990.

Thomas, Roy, Gary Friedrich (writers), and Mike Ploog (artist). *Marvel Spotlight,* #5. "A Legend Is Born." New York: Marvel, August 1972.

Thomas, Roy, Dann Thomas (writers), Don Newton, and Tim Burgard (artists). *Infinity, Inc.,* #31. "Press Conference." New York: DC, March 1985.

Tobin, Paul (writer), Clayton Henry, and Pepe Larraz (artists). *Spider-Girl: Family Values,* #1. New York: Marvel, January 2011.

Tobin, Paul (writer), and Pepe Larraz (artist). *Spider-Island: The Amazing Spider-Girl,* vol. 1, #1. "Class Warfare." New York: Marvel, October 2011.

Van Lente, Fred (writer), Wellinton Alves, and Pere Pérez (artists). *Power Man and Iron Fist.* "The Comedy of Death." New York: Marvel, 2011.

Vaughan, Brian K. (writer), and Adrian Alphona (artist). *Runaways,* #1. New York: Marvel, July 2003.

Velez, Ivan, Jr., Dwayne McDuffie (writers), and Treveor Von Eden (artist). *Blood Syndicate,* #2. "America Eats Its Young." New York: Milestone, 1993.

Velez, Ivan Jr. (writer), and CrissCross (artist). *Blood Syndicate*, #13. "Dressed to Kill." New York: Milestone, April 1994.

Wein, Len (writer), Chuck Patton, and Del Barras (artists). *Blue Beetle*, vol. 1, #10. New York: DC, March 1987.

Williams, Rob (writer), Matthew Clark, Brian Ching (artists). *Ghost Rider*, vol. 7, #1. "Fear Itself." New York: Marvel, April–October 2011.

Winick, Judd (writer), and Guillem March (artist). *Catwoman, Vol. 1: The Game*. New York: DC, May 2012.

Winnick, Judd (writer), and Keith Giffen (artist). *Justice League: Generation Lost*, #1. New York: DC, July 2010.

Wilson, G. Willow (writer) and Adrian Alphona (artist). *Ms. Marvel*, vol. 1. New York: Marvel, 2014.

Wolfman, Marv (writer), George Pérez, and Dick Giordano (artists). *Crisis on Infinite Earths*, #6. New York: DC, September 1986.

Wolfman, Marv (writer), and Jerry Ordway (artist). *Adventures of Superman*, #428. "Personal Best." New York: DC, May 1987.

Wolfman, Marv (writer), and Tom Grindberg (artist). *New Teen Titans Annual*, vol. 1, #7. New York: DC, 1991.

Wolfman, Marv (writer), and Tom Grummett (artist). *New Titans*, #73. "Paradise Lost." New York: DC, February 1991.

Animation

Bendis, Brian Michael, and Paul Dini. *Ultimate Spider-Man*. Marvel Animation, 2012–2016.

De le Peña, Adam. *Minoriteam*. Adult Swim, 2005–2006.

Do Santos, Joaquim, and Dan Riba. *Justice League Unlimited*. Cartoon Network, 2004–2006.

Gutierrez, Jorge. *El Tigre*. Nickelodeon, 2008.

Haskell, Barkin, and Dick Conway. *Super Friends*. ABC, 1981.

Lee, Stan, and Marv Wolfman. *The Condor*. Cartoon Network, 2007.

Pérez, George, Marv Wolfman, and Arnold Drake. *Teen Titans Go!* "Más Y Menos." Cartoon Network. Season 1, episode 48, April 2014.

Tucker, James, and Michael Jelenic. *Batman: Brave and the Bold*. Cartoon Network, 2008–2011.

Wolfram, Amy and Ben Jones. *Teen Titans*. "Calling All Titans." Cartoon Network. Episode 63, January 7, 2006.

Alcalá, Félix Enríquez and Lorne Cameron. *Justice League of America.* "Pilot." CBS, 1997.

Berlanti, Greg, and Andrew Kreisberg. *Legends of Tomorrow.* CW, 2016– .

———. *Supergirl.* CBS, 2015– .

Berlanti, Greg, Andrew Kreisberg, and Geoff Johns. *The Flash.* CW, 2014– .

———. *The Flash.* "Chronicles of Cisco." CW, April 20, 2016. Web. Accessed December 21, 2016. https://www.youtube.com/watch?v =0ACubCvAyWA.

———. *The Flash.* "The Chronicles of Cisco." Blog. CW, May 20– December 5, 2016. Web. Accessed December 21, 2016. http:// chroniclesofcisco.tumblr.com/.

Cameron, James. *Dark Angel.* Fox, 2000–2002.

Cannon, Danny. *Gotham.* Fox, 2014– .

Echevaría, Reneé. "Freak Nation." Fox, May 2012.

Edlund, Ben, and Barry Sonnenfeld. *The Tick.* "Pilot." Fox, November 8, 2001.

Goddard, Drew. *Daredevil.* Netflix, April 10, 2015.

Gough, Alfred, and Miles Millar. *Smallville.* "Angel of Vengeance." CW. Season 5, episode 13, February 2006.

———. *Smallville.* "Booster." CW. Season 10, episode 18, April 2011.

Kring, Tim. *Heroes.* "Four Months Later . . ." NBC. Season 2, episode 1, September 24, 2007.

———. *Heroes: Reborn.* NBC, 2015–2016.

Rosenberg, Melissa. *Jessica Jones.* Netflix, November 20, 2015.

Whedon, Joss. *Agents of S.H.I.E.L.D.* ABC. Season 1, episode 2, October 2013.

———. *Agents of S.H.I.E.L.D.: Slingshot.* Web. Accessed December 20, 2016. http://abc.go.com/shows/marvels-agents-of-shield-slingshot.

Films

Ayer, David. *Suicide Squad.* Warner Brothers, 2016.

Branagh, Kenneth. *Thor.* Marvel Studios, 2011.

Cameron, James. *Avatar,* 20th Century Fox, 2009.

Campell, Martin. *Green Lantern.* Warner Brothers, 2011.

Del Toro, Guillermo. *Blade II.* Marvel Entertainment, 2002.

Derrickson, Scott. *Dr. Strange*. Marvel Studios, 2016.

Dippé, Mark A. Z. *Spawn*. New Line Cinema, 1997.

Gunn, James. *Guardians of the Galaxy*. Marvel Studios, 2014.

Hayward, Jimmy. *Jonah Hex*. Warner Brothers, 2010.

Hensleigh, Jonathan. *The Punisher*. Marvel Enterprises, 2004.

Hood, Gavin. *The Wolverine*, 20th Century Fox, 2009.

———. *X-Men Origins: Wolverine*. Marvel Entertainment, 2009.

Johnson, Kenneth. *Steel*. Warner Brothers, 1997.

Johnson, Mark Steven. *Ghost Rider*. Columbia Pictures, 2007.

Johnston, Joe. *Captain America: The First Avenger*. Marvel Studios, 2011.

Mangold, James. *Logan*. Marvel Entertainment, 2017.

Megaton, Olivier. *Colombiana*. EuropaCorp, 2011.

Nolan, Christopher. *Batman Begins*. Warner Brothers, 2005.

———. *Dark Knight Rises*. Warner Brothers, 2012.

Norrington, Stephen. *Blade*. Marvel Entertainment, 1998.

Pitof. *Catwoman*. Warner Brothers, 2004.

Reed, Peyton. *Ant-Man*. Marvel Studios, 2015.

Singer, Bryan. *X-Men*. Marvel Entertainment, 2000.

———. *X2-X-Men United*. Marvel Enterprises, 2003.

Snyder, Zack. *Batman v. Superman: Dawn of Justice*. Warner Bros, 2016.

Townsend, Robert. *The Meteor Man*. Metro-Goldwyn-Mayer, 1993.

Vaughn, Matthew. *X-Men: First Class*. Marvel Entertainment, 2011.

INDEX

Latino superheroes: gay; lesbian
superheroes
geometric shapes, xvi–xvii, 59–60,
96–97, 108, 116
geometric shaping, 70, 95, 120,
179. *See also* shaping devices:
geometric
geometrizing, 5, 174–75; of Latina
superheroes, 22, 28, 61; of Latino
storyworlds, 17, 95, 180; of
Latino superheroes, 35, 73, 76,
87, 89, 108, 116, 173; of story, 18,
20, 39, 41, 90, 94–99, 111, 114,
118, 121, 123, 127, 174, 183
geometry, 18, 60, 116; storyfying
of, 41, 114–16, 123, 127
gestalt, 99, 102, 114
Ghost Rider, 9, 48, 60, 81–82, 122,
142, 150, 151*f*, 173, 183
Giffen, Keith, 22, 73, 122, 173
Gillen, Kieron, 85–86
Glass, Adam, 32, 157
Gleason, Patrick, 70, 122
Global Guardians, 21–22
Goodwin, Archie, 34–35
Gotham Central, 60, 88
Gough, Alfred, 137–38
Green Fury (Green Flame/Fire),
21–22, 23*f*, 28, 128
Green Lantern, 45, 75, 110, 156
El Guapo (Robbie Rodriguez), 63–66
Guara, Ig, 73, 99, 106–8
Guttierrez, Jorge, 128, 134–36, 173

Haghenbeck, F. G., 54, 56
Hamilton, Edmond, 14–15
Hawkgirl, 132, 139
Hayward, Jimmy, 151–53
Henry, Clayton, 68, 111, 113*f*
Hernandez, Jaime, 95, 175–77
Hernandez, Javier, 93, 95, 175
Hero Cruz, 45–46, 75
Heroes, 146–49
Hester, Phil, 32, 122

Imán, 54–56
independent comics, xii, 35, 181
inkers, 26, 91, 95, 98, 104, 116

Johns, Geoff, 37, 58, 60, 74–75, 143
Jonah Hex (Hayward), 151, 152*f*,
153*f*
Jones, Gerard, 31–32, 122
Justice League of America, 9, 22, 58
Justice League of America's Vibe,
87, 88*f*, 104, 105*f*, 117*f*, 118

Kirby, Jack, 11–12, 95–96, 165, 175
Kreisberg, Andrew, 86–87, 138–39,
143
Kring, Tim, 146–48

Latina superheroes, 8, 21–23,
27–28, 34–37, 44, 50–51, 54,
57–58, 60–62, 66–68, 73–75,
85–86, 94, 120–21, 128, 131,
134, 137, 139–41, 145, 166, 170,
173, 175–78
Latinidad, 3, 19, 22, 68, 118–19,
121, 138–39; Afro-Brazilian, 24
Latino superheroes, 3–9, 16–18,
20, 29, 31, 37–38, 42–45, 48–49,
53–54, 56–57, 59, 66, 70, 72, 85,
87, 89, 92, 95, 99, 104, 112–13,
124, 126–28, 148, 173, 175,
179–83; in animation, 128–36;
bildungsroman narratives and,
8, 39, 41, 43, 51, 52*f*, 122, 146;
bilingualism and, 18, 20, 28,
54, 64, 76, 83, 119; Caucasian-
featured, 122; and complexity of
character, 16, 29, 73, 87, 94, 97,
118, 121, 157, 160, 182; creators
of, xviii; disabled, 47, 51, 134;
erasure of, 6; in film, 156, 159,
169–71; gay, 3, 29, 36, 42, 75, 78;
geometrizing of, 90; Latinidad
and, 118; light-skinned, 4, 11,
21, 39, 44, 71, 121; racism and,
26–27; as self-taught, 29, 41,
43, 56, 119, 123; on television,
xv, xix, 3–4, 6, 92, 96, 124, 127,
136–40, 142–44, 146, 149, 170–
72, 173–74, 179; urban, 22, 27,
34–36; vigilantism and, 34–35;
visual representation of, 111,
123. *See also* Latina superheroes

ABOUT THE AUTHOR

Frederick Luis Aldama is the Arts and Humanities Distinguished Professor of English and a University Distinguished Scholar at the Ohio State University. He is founder and director of LASER, a mentoring and research hub for Latinos (ninth grade through college), which was selected as a 2015 Bright Spot in Hispanic Education by the White House Initiative on Educational Excellence for Hispanics. An expert on Latino popular culture, Aldama is the author, co-author, and editor of twenty-six books, including *Your Brain on Latino Comics: From Gus Arriola to Los Bros Hernandez* and *The Cinema of Robert Rodriguez.*